WEB DESIGN: PORTFOLIOS

Ed. Julius Wiedemann

TASCHEN

HONGKONG KÖLN LONDON LOS ANGELES MADRID PARIS TOKYO

Los mejores porfolios están en la red

Como editor, no dejo de buscar fuentes de consulta para las obras que coordino. Con el paso de los años he llegado a la conclusión de que existe un lugar donde se encuentra todo lo que se necesita: Internet. Sin embargo, hay que saber cómo buscar la información para no perder un tiempo precioso. De eso precisamente trata este libro: usted quiere lo mejor en cuanto a navegación, gráficos, programación, etc., y esta obra es la fuente de consulta de pequeño formato que necesita para adquirir servicios, asesorar a sus clientes, inspirarse y entrar en contacto con ideas nuevas. Hemos recopilado 200 porfolios de más de 30 países distintos para ofrecer una amplia visión del panorama actual, pero ni el libro ni la diversión terminan ahí: los porfolios incluyen vínculos a páginas igual de interesantes, empezando por las de los diseñadores y estudios que los crearon.

Observará que el libro se concentra en ámbitos creativos, lo cual responde a una serie de razones. En primer lugar, son los ámbitos en los que se emplea el término «porfolio», es decir, el lugar donde se muestra una obra con la intención de atraer y entretener a potenciales clientes y visitantes en general. En segundo lugar, las disciplinas artísticas, como la fotografía, la ilustración o el diseño gráfico, muchas veces requieren (o desean tener como valor añadido) soluciones específicas para realizar las obras expuestas. En tercer lugar, despliegan mucha más libertad creativa, pues no tienen las limitaciones

de una imagen corporativa o de unos estándares determinados para los vínculos. Todo eso permite un mayor grado de experimentación, que a menudo conlleva el descubrimiento de nuevos e imaginativos modos de navegar, exponer (y disponer) las obras y, finalmente, captar la atención de los visitantes.

Durante la elaboración de este libro me di cuenta de que los fotógrafos están dando un paso adelante para crear (y costearse) extraordinarios porfolios en línea. Por eso, si se dedica a la fotografía y aún no está en Internet, dese prisa. Por otro lado, creo que es lógico que los diseñadores gráficos dispongan de magníficos sitios web, pues tienen especial interés en exponer lo mejor de sus trabajos y casi siempre crean sus porfolios ellos mismos. Incluso hay diseñadores que simplemente se sirven de su web para mostrar su potencial creativo. Por último, hay muchos profesionales que consideran que Internet es el medio del presente, no el del futuro. Pensar que la red es la puerta de acceso a la atención del mundo es creer en la importancia de este nuevo medio y en su capacidad para cambiar la vida de quienes lo utilizan.

Merece la pena prestar atención no sólo a los porfolios, sino también a las personas que los han elaborado. Me permito recordar aquí que uno de los grandes avances de nuestra época es la práctica desaparición de la distancia entre proveedor y cliente: todo está en la red y todo es cuestión de software. Un viaje por los sitios web de los creadores de los porfolios resultará igual de estimulante que el paseo por las páginas de este libro. Además, en esta obra se ofrece información que suele ser difícil de encontrar en ningún otro sitio, como el precio por hora y los datos de contacto de los diseñadores, o los créditos de los programadores. Estos últimos son corresponsables de esta revolución y, sin embargo, casi nunca se les menciona ni se reconoce su contribución, aunque son ellos quienes saben mejor que nadie el reto que supone llevar a la práctica una idea nueva.

El proceso de selección previo a la elaboración de un libro de estas características no es sencillo. En primer lugar, porque la cantidad de material disponible es prácticamente infinita, ya que no sólo todos los días se publican nuevos sitios web sino que también se rediseñan los ya existentes. En segundo lugar, no nos limitamos a publicar lo que nos envían ni aceptamos que nos paguen por aparecer en la obra. Así el libro gana en calidad, pues se ofrece al lector una selección de primera clase y no la de una serie de personas que podían pagar su inclusión. También se consigue que resulte más estimulante, que es nuestro principal objetivo. También hemos buscado porfolios premiados, aunque no considerábamos que fuera lo más importante.

Verá que la mayoría de los porfolios han sido realizados con Flash, lo que en mi opinión es natural.

Se puede objetar que así verlos lleva más tiempo, pero hay que tener en cuenta que en Internet la paciencia es una virtud, y además las conexiones cada vez son mejores. Durante mis viajes he tenido ocasión de conectarme en varios países, por lo que soy consciente de la diferencia de velocidad de un lugar a otro. Pero considero que, a pesar de ese pequeño inconveniente del Flash, lo importante es la calidad del material elegido.

Puede que se pregunte (y que desee preguntarme a mí) por qué esta obra se publica en papel. Podríamos publicarla en Internet, pero al dar forma de libro proporcionamos una fuente de consulta portátil e instantánea que se puede llevar encima. Con la extensión de las conexiones inalámbricas es cada vez más sencillo conectarse en cualquier lugar, pero aun así las obras impresas siguen teniendo razón de ser.

Desde aquí animamos a todo el mundo a conectarse a Internet y visitar los sitios web en su contexto. Cuando usted lo haga, lo estará haciendo ya con su propio criterio de selección. Así que... ¡adelante!

Julius Wiedemann

I portfolio migliori sono on-line

In qualità d'editore sono sempre alla ricerca delle fonti bibliografiche per le pubblicazioni che curo. Dopo anni d'esperienze, posso affermare che c'è un solo posto dove poter trovare tutto ciò che mi serve: il Web. Bisogna, tuttavia, sapere dove cercare per non perdere tempo prezioso. Da qui l'utilità di questo libro. Se volete conoscere il meglio sulla navigazione, la grafica, la programmazione, eccetera, è la risorsa bibliografica essenziale da usare per acquistare servizi, come guida per i clienti, come ispirazione e stimolo. Abbiamo raccolto 200 portfolio di più di 30 paesi per fornire un ampio quadro delle risorse disponibili. Il libro e il divertimento, però, non si esauriscono qui: si possono consultare anche le pagine collegate ai siti indicati, compresi quelle dei designer e delle strutture che li hanno progettati.

E' evidente che il libro focalizza lo sguardo sui settori della creatività, per una serie di motivi logici. Prima di tutto, è proprio in questi settori che si usa il termine "portfolio", che rappresenta la vetrina dei prodotti realizzati ed è finalizzata a pubblicizzare o divertire i potenziali clienti e i semplici visitatori. In secondo luogo, settori come la fotografia, l'illustrazione, il graphic design e così via, richiedono molto spesso (o è desiderabile che abbiano come marcia in più) delle soluzioni specifiche per valorizzare il lavoro esposto. Terzo, hanno una maggiore libertà di creazione senza essere condizionati da un'immagine aziendale o avere vincoli di particolari standard, il che permette una

maggiore sperimentazione e spesso l'individuazione di nuovi strumenti di navigazione, oltre a mettere in mostra (e in gioco) le opere e, infine, catturare l'attenzione degli spettatori in modi impensabili in linea di principio.

Nel curare la realizzazione di questo libro, sono giunto alla conclusione che i fotografi sono un passo avanti nel creare (e pagare) grandiose vetrine on-line. Se lavorate in questo settore e non avete ancora un sito, affrettatevi. È certo comprensibile che i disegnatori grafici abbiano dei bei siti, perché hanno un interesse diretto a mettere in mostra il proprio lavoro al meglio. E sono, per lo più, capaci di farlo da soli. Alcuni usano persino il loro sito solo per mostrare le loro capacità creative. E, alla fine, c'è chi crede che Internet sia il mezzo di comunicazione del presente, e non del futuro. Credere che il Web sia la chiave per catalizzare l'attenzione del pubblico, significa credere nell'importanza e nella differenza che questo mezzo può rappresentare nella vita professionale.

Nella lettura di questo libro si dovrà fare attenzione non solo ai portfolio ma anche a chi li ha realizzati. Bisogna sempre ricordare che, ai nostri giorni, la cosa più positiva è che non c'è virtualmente nessuna distanza tra produttore e acquirente. È tutto on-line ed è tutto software. Una visita ai siti produttori si dimostrerà un viaggio pieno d'ispirazioni, così come navigare all'interno di questo libro, in cui troverete anche una serie di dati difficili da trovare altrimenti, inclusi i costi in ore, i contatti dei designer e i credits dei programmatori. Questi ultimi, raramente menzionati in pubblicazioni del genere, di solito non ricevono adeguato credito come corresponsabili di questa rivoluzione. Loro sanno quali sono le difficoltà che devono affrontare nel mettere in pratica una nuova idea.

Il processo di selezione di un libro di questo genere non è per nulla facile. Prima di tutto perché l'insieme dei materiali a disposizione è, per certi aspetti, infinito, poiché non solo si mettono in rete quotidianamente nuovi siti ma li aggiornano anche. Secondo, il nostro lavoro non è sovvenzionato o pagato, il che rende il libro più ricco, in quanto il lettore ha a disposizione una selezione di prima scelta e non solo un insieme di nomi che possono permettserlo. Tutto ciò lo rende ancora più interessante. Non ce ne stanchiamo mai. Abbiamo anche cercato chi fosse stato premiato per il suo lavoro, anche se non è stato il fattore di scelta principale. Si noterà che la maggior parte dei siti sono realizzati con Flash e io penso che sia la soluzione naturale. Si potrebbe obiettare sul tempo necessario per visualizzare una pagina, ma la pazienza è una virtù nella rete e le connessioni migliorano sempre di più. Mi connetto a Internet in diversi paesi durante i miei viaggi e sono consapevole delle differenze tra i servizi a disposizione. Alla fine, ciò che importa è la qualità del materiale selezionato.

Ci si potrebbe chiedere perché è necessario avere una versione a stampa. Potrebbe benissimo funzionare on-line ma così si ha a disposizione una bibliografia portatile per la consultazione immediata. Con il diffondersi delle connessioni wireless diventa facile connettersi in qualunque posto. Una bibliografia scritta è, però, ancora uno strumento validissimo. Incoraggiamo tutti a provare on-line i siti consigliati e, quando lo farete, ci riuscirete facilmente con in nostri criteri di selezione. Forza!

Julius Wiedemann

Os melhores portfólios estão online

Como editor, estou constantemente à procura de referências para todas as publicações em que estive envolvido. Após alguns anos, cheguei à conclusão de que apenas existe um sítio onde posso encontrar tudo aquilo de que preciso: a Web. Mas é fundamental que se saiba de antemão o que se procura, para não perder, deste modo, horas preciosas até encontrar as referências necessárias. E este livro é importante precisamente neste aspecto. Se pretender dispor do melhor que existe em termos de navegação, gráficos, programação, etc., necessita de uma referência compacta como esta, que o ajudará a procurar um determinado serviço e servirá como referência para clientes, como inspiração e desafio. Seleccionámos 200 portfólios oriundos de mais de 30 países, de forma a dar-lhe uma visão ampla sobre o que está a acontecer no mundo da Web. Mas o livro e o prazer que este lhe proporcionará vão mais longe, já que os links indicados lhe permitem ainda visitar variadíssimos sites de enorme qualidade, incluindo os designers e as agências que os conceberam.

Terá a oportunidade de ver que este livro incide sobre as áreas criativas, o que se explica pelas seguintes razões: em primeiro lugar, trata-se de áreas em que as pessoas utilizam realmente o termo portfólio, elemento essencial para apresentar uma produção, com o objectivo de fazer publicidade ou divertir potenciais clientes e outros visitantes. Em segundo lugar, as áreas criativas, tal como a fotografia, a ilustração, o design gráfico, entre outras, exigem muitas vezes soluções específicas (ou é

esperado que as tenham, de forma a distinguirem-se das restantes) para realçar o trabalho apresentado. Por fim, beneficiam de uma muito maior liberdade para criar sem se preocuparem com a imagem corporativa ou ligações a padrões específicos. Isto permite-lhes fazer experiências inovadoras, descobrir muitas vezes novos modos de navegar e de apresentar trabalhos (e jogar com estes), com vista a captar a atenção dos utilizadores de uma forma que, em princípio, não seria imaginável.

Ao trabalhar neste livro, cheguei à conclusão de que os fotógrafos estão a dar um passo em frente e a criar (e a pagar por isso) apresentações online extremamente entusiasmantes. Portanto, se trabalha nesta área e não se encontra online, é melhor despachar-se. A meu ver, não é de estranhar que os designers gráficos tenham excelentes sites, na medida em que são aqueles que, por um lado, estão directamente interessados em apresentar da melhor forma o seu trabalho e, por outro, são os mais competentes para o fazer. Existem mesmo alguns designers que apenas utilizam o seu site para demonstrar a sua capacidade criativa. Por fim, existem ainda todos aqueles que acreditam que a Internet constitui o meio do momento e não do futuro. Acreditar na Web como um meio para captar a atenção das pessoas é acreditar na sua importância e na diferença que pode representar para a vida destes profissionais.

Uma coisa a ter em atenção neste livro, além do portfólio, são as pessoas que nele colaboraram.

Deve ser relembrado que a melhor coisa hoje em dia é o facto de não existirem basicamente distâncias entre o produtor e o comprador. Tudo está disponível online e tudo é software. Uma visita aos criadores dos sites irá certamente ser muito inspiradora. Tanto quanto a navegação por este livro. Também poderá encontrar aqui um conjunto de parâmetros, raramente encontrados em publicações do género, incluindo os preços que são cobrados por hora. Nesta obra, são indicados ainda os contactos dos designers e os créditos para os programadores. Estes últimos, raramente mencionados nas publicações, são co-responsáveis por esta verdadeira revolução, e poucas vezes obtêm o reconhecimento merecido. São eles que assumem o verdadeiro desafio quando é necessário pôr em prática ideias novas.

O processo de selecção para um livro destes não é nada fácil. Antes de mais, porque o material disponível para ser avaliado é, de certo modo, infinito, porque não só são criados diariamente novos sites, mas também porque os antigos são constantemente recriados. Em segundo lugar, não estamos submetidos a ninguém nem aceitamos pagamentos. Isto enriqueceu o presente projecto, pois o leitor tem ao seu dispor uma selecção de grande qualidade e não apenas um grupo de pessoas que se podem dar ao luxo de serem apresentadas. Mas, ao mesmo tempo, também representa um desafio acrescido, que enfrentámos com grande entusiasmo. Também tivemos em consideração os projectos que obtiveram prémios

nesta categoria, sem que, no entanto, seja este aspecto o nosso objectivo primordial. Terá a oportunidade de ver que a maior parte dos trabalhos são feitos em Flash, o que considero facilmente compreensível. Pode-se contrapor que esta opção obriga a um maior tempo de espera até conseguir ver a página, mas, no mundo da Internet, a paciência é muitas vezes uma virtude. Além disso, as ligações têm vindo a ser cada vez mais rápidas. Durante as minhas viagens, navego pela Internet em vários países e estou a par das diferenças que existem e dos serviços disponíveis. Mas o mais importante acaba sempre por ser a qualidade do material seleccionado.

Poderá interrogar-se (e a mim também) sobre a necessidade de uma publicação sobre este tema. Bem, também poderíamos ter feito um site sobre o assunto, mas, com este livro, pomos à sua disposição um meio de referência móvel e imediato que poderá levar sempre consigo. À medida que as ligações sem fios vão sendo mais e mais populares, a possibilidade de estar online em qualquer lado tem-se tornado cada vez mais fácil. Mas, a verdade é que uma referência impressa continua a ser fundamental. Encorajamo-lo a ir à Internet para apreciar os sites online. E, ao entrar neste mundo, irá sem dúvida fazê-lo com os seus próprios critérios de escolha. Aproveite a oportunidade!

Julius Wiedemann

3:AM DESIGN

www.3am-design.com

Concept

La cafeína es una cruel amante. //// *La caffeina è una padrona severa.* //// **A cafeína é uma amante severa..**

Infos

DESIGN: 3:AM Design Inc. /// **PROGRAMMING:** Jody Poole. /// **AWARDS:** the World Heavyweight Belt. /// **TOOLS:** html, Macromedia Flash, Quicktime, Adobe Affter Effects. /// **COST:** 25 hours. /// **MAINTENANCE:** 2 hours per month.

808INC.

www.808inc.com

Concept

Presentación organizada, intuitiva y con cuerpo de contenidos creativos en varios formatos. //// *Una presentazione essenziale e intuitiva di contenuti creativi formattati in modi diversi.* //// **Apresentação de corpo inteiro, orgânica, intuitiva, de conteúdos criativos formatados de diversas formas.**

Infos

DESIGN: Joshua Davis <www.joshuadavis.com> and The Department of Notation. /// **PROGRAMMING:** Branden Hall (The Department of Notation). /// **TOOLS:** Macromedia Flash. /// **COST:** $50K. /// **MAINTENANCE:** 3 hours per month.

3RD EDGE COMMUNICATIONS

www.3rdedge.com

Concept

Nuestra aproximación al diseño queda patente en la hermosa simplicidad de esta web. //// Il nostro approccio al design si rivela nella semplice bellezza del sito. //// A nossa abordagem ao design revela-se na bonita simplicidade deste site.

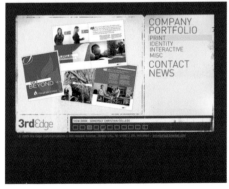

Infos

DESIGN: 3rd Edge Communications. /// **PROGRAMMING:** Manny Dilone. /// **TOOLS:** html, Macromedia Flash. /// **COST:** 120-140 hours /// **MAINTENANCE:** 4 hours per month.

417NORTH

www.417north.com

Concept

Sencilla y austera. Intuitiva y personal. //// *Semplice e chiaro. Intuitivo e personale.* //// **Simples e claro. Intuitivo e pessoal.**

Infos

DESIGN AND PROGRAMMING: Greg Huntoon (Go Farm) <www.gofarm.la>. /// AWARDS: Reboot Winner, TINY (Site of the Month), FWA (Site of the Day). /// TOOLS: Macromedia Flash, xml. /// COST: 200 hours. /// MAINTENANCE: 5–10 hours per month.

Concept

Mientras hay negrura, hay esperanza. //// Finché c'è vita c'è speranza. //// Quanto mais preto houver, mais esperança irá encontrar.

Infos

DESIGN: RUN (Semper Fi) <www.semperultimo.com>. /// **PROGRAMMING:** Bens and GUS (Semper Fi). /// **AWARDS:** Flash Forward, Flash Festival. ///
TOOLS: Macromedia Flash. /// **COST:** 130 hours. /// **MAINTENANCE:** 1 hour per month.

Concept

Una presentación elegante y discreta de un amplio conjunto de obras que no distrae la atención de la auténtica razón de ser de la web. ////
Una presentazione elegante e minimale di un vasto corpus di lavori che in ogni caso riesce a non distrarre dal centro d'attenzione del sito. ////
Uma apresentação elegante e minimalista da obra do artista que não distrai do elemento principal do site.

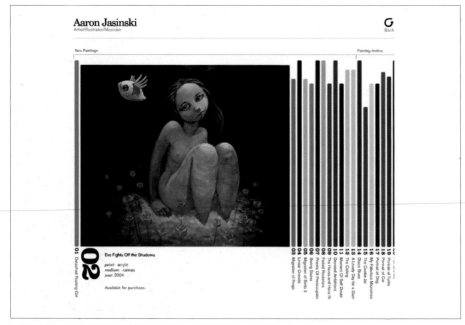

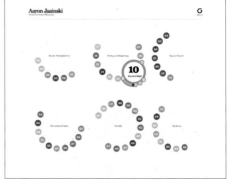

Infos

DESIGN: Craig Erickson (Section Seven) <www.sectionseven.com>. /// **PROGRAMMING:** Jason Keimig. /// **AWARDS:** TINY (Featured Site), FWA (Site Of The Day), TAXI (Site of the Day). /// **TOOLS:** Macromedia Flash. /// **COST:** 100 hours. /// **MAINTENANCE:** 0–5 hours per month.

ACHT FRANKFURT

www.acht-frankfurt.de

Concept

La web corporativa de la empresa de postproducción Acht Frankfurt combina videos e interactividad en Internet. El porfolio actual se presenta en forma de reproductor interactivo dinámico. //// La pagina web per la compagnia di post produzione 'Acht Frankfurt' unisce il principio cinematografico e l'interattività della rete. L'attuale portfolio si presenta sotto forma di uno showreel interattivo e dinamico. //// O site da empresa de pós-produção Acht Frankfurt combina os princípios do cinema com a interactividade da Net. O portfólio actual da empresa é apresentado como Showreel dinâmico.

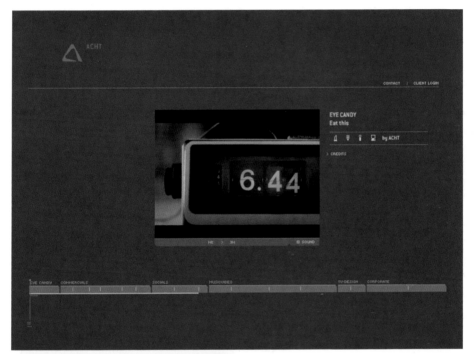

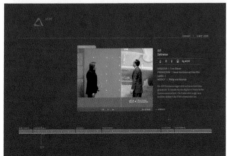

Infos

DESIGN: Scholz & Volkmer <www.s-v.de>. /// **PROGRAMMING:** Duc-Thuan Bui and Manfred Kraft. /// **AWARDS:** Art Directors Club Berlin, Best of Business-to-Business-Award (Bonn), Golden Awards (Montreux), Clio, One Show Interactive, Cannes Cyber Lion, iF Communication Design, I.D. Interactive Media Design Review, and more. /// **TOOLS:** html, Macromedia Flash, xml, music, film. /// **COST:** n/a. /// **MAINTENANCE:** n/a.

ACIDTWIST GALLERY

www.acidtwist.com

Concept

La idea de partida era tomarse la expresión «galería de imágenes» al pie de la letra: la inspiraron fotografías de paredes de galerías de arte. //// L'idea fondamentale era prendere alla lettera l'espressione "galleria d'immagini" e trarre ispirazione da fotografie di musei d'arte. //// O conceito subjacente consistia em tomar à letra a frase "galeria de imagens" – inspirado em fotografias de muros com obras de arte.

Infos

DESIGN: Tavish (Acidtwist). /// TOOLS: Macromedia Flash, xml, html. /// COST: 60 hours. /// MAINTENANCE: 1-2 hours per month. New images are uploaded to a folder on the server, and their filenames are added to an xml file. The Flash front-end adapts automatically to the image dimensions.

AERIFORM VISCOM

www.aeriform.co.uk

Concept

Se recurrió al lenguaje gráfico de los mapas y al uso de colores intensos y complementarios para crear una web impactante pero a la vez sencilla. //// Il linguaggio grafico delle mappe unite a colori audaci e ed elogiativi è stato impiegato per creare un sito straordinario benché semplice. //// Recorreu-se à linguagem gráfica dos mapas, aliada a cores fortes e complementares, de forma a criar um site que atrai a atenção, apesar da sua simplicidade.

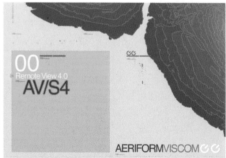

Infos

DESIGN AND PROGRAMMING: Aeriform Viscom. /// TOOLS: html, Macromedia Flash. /// COST: 48 hours per month.

ACTIVATE.RU

www.activate.ru

RUSSIA

2004

Concept

Algo positivo, directo y emocional. La idea básica consistía en dar mi punto de vista sobre la función del diseño contemporáneo. //// Positivo, immediato ed emozionante... L'idea principale è quella di spiegare la mia visione della missione del design contemporaneo. //// Algo positivo, sincero e emocional... A principal ideia consistiu em explicar a minha visão da missão contemporânea do design.

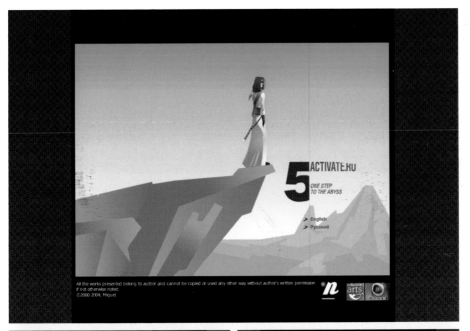

Infos

DESIGN AND PROGRAMMING: Mikhail Ivanov. /// AWARDS: Netdiver Design Forte, ComputerSpace, and several minor awards. /// TOOLS: html, Macromedia Flash. /// COST: 50-60 hours. /// MAINTENANCE: several hours per month to upload new images and update information.

MONSIEUR A

www.adenek.com

Concept

Una búsqueda que concede gran importancia a lo visual, con un diseño absorbente. //// Il sito è una ricerca per dare risalto all'elemento visivo attraverso la realizzazione di un design immersive. //// Determinado a dar uma grande importância ao aspecto visual, criando um design visualmente imergente.

Infos

DESIGN AND PROGRAMMING: Mathieu Zylberait [Monsieur A]. /// AWARDS: Moluv's Picks, Plasticpilots, Netdiver, DOPE, NewWebPick. /// TOOLS: Macromedia Flash. /// COST: 2 weeks. /// MAINTENANCE: 2 hours per month.

AD PLANET

www.adplanet.com.sg

Concept

La atmósfera de la web es intensa, inspiradora y emotiva, como reflejo de un cliente profundamente orgulloso de sus raíces (singapurenses) y de sus logros. //// Il clima del sito web è forte, ispirato ed emotivo, per riflettere l'immagine di un cliente che va molto fiero delle proprie origini locali (Singapore) nonché delle sue conquiste. //// O site caracteriza-se por um ambiente forte, inspirador e emotivo, de forma a reflectir um cliente extremamente orgulloso das suas raízes locais (singapurense) e das suas realizações.

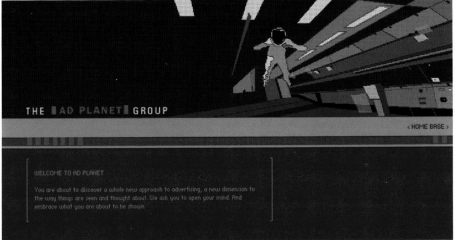

Infos

DESIGN: Kinetic Interactive <www.kinetic.com.sg>. /// PROGRAMMING: Sean Lam. /// AWARDS: One Show Interactive, New York Festival, Singapore Creative Circle, FWA. /// TOOLS: Macromedia Flash, Macromedia Dreamweaver, Adobe Photoshop, Soundedit. /// COST: 70 hours. /// MAINTENANCE: 1 hour per month.

ALBERT BOULLET

www.albert.st

Concept

La web se hizo lo más minimalista posible para que las fotografías fueran el elemento principal y constituyeran el diseño por sí mismas. //// Il sito è ridotto al minimo in modo da rendere le fotografie l'elemento principale e costituire da sole il design. //// O site foi concebido da forma mais minimal possível para que a atenção recaia apenas nos fotógrafos, sendo eles próprios o design.

Infos

DESIGN: Screenplay <www.screenplay.no>, and Hei <www.hei.no>. /// **AWARDS:** Web by Visuel (Gold - Best Presentation). /// **TOOLS:** Macromedia Flash, xml. /// **COST:** no cost, exchanged jobs. /// **MAINTENANCE:** no cost, I maintain the site myself.

ALLEN VENABLES PHOTO

www.allenvenables.com

Concept

Para exponer el porfolio de Allen Venables teníamos que reflejar de algún modo su agudo sentido del humor. //// Per la presentazione del portfolio di Allen Venables è stato necessario catturare in qualche modo il senso asciutto dell'umorismo di Allen. //// Para apresentar o portfólio de Allen Venables tivemos que encontrar uma forma de captar o sentido de humor seco de Allen.

Infos

DESIGN: Ren Spiteri (Virtual Bulldog) <www.virtualbulldog.com>. /// **AWARDS:** Bombshock, FWA, Best Website Award, Worldwide Web Awards. /// **TOOLS:** Macromedia Flash. /// **COST:** 1 month.

MY EYES, YOUR WORLD
www.amivitale.com

Concept

Un porfolio rápido y austero en el que las imágenes tienen toda la prioridad y el sistema de navegación invita a explorarlas. //// Ecco un portfolio veloce e senza difetti in cui le immagini hanno la precedenza e la navigazione invita l'utente all'esplorazione. //// Um portfólio rápido e claro em que a primazia é dada às imagens e a navegação convida o visitante a explorar os recantos.

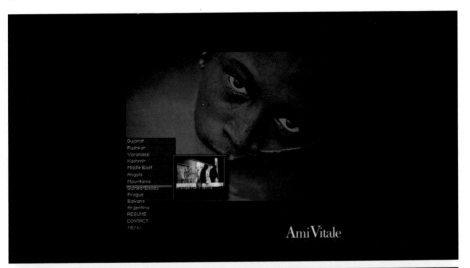

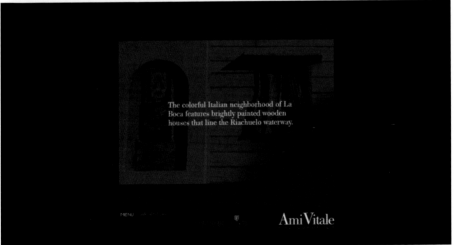

Infos

DESIGN AND PROGRAMMING: Jayson Singe (Neon Sky Creative Media) <www.neonsky.com>. /// AWARDS: Photo District News "PIX" Digital Imaging Competition (Best Site), Flash Film Festival Amsterdam, Flash Forward. /// TOOLS: Macromedia Flash, html, Adobe Photoshop, Apple Final Cut Pro. /// COST: 100 hours. /// MAINTENANCE: 1 hour per month.

ANATOL KOTTE

www.anatolkotte.com

GERMANY

2004

Concept

El diseño y la navegación minimalistas de la web aportan dinamismo y vida a los contenidos. //// Il design e la navigazione essenziali del sito conferiscono dinamicità ai contenuti e aggiungono un'impressione di vita. //// O design e a navegação minimalistas dinamizam o conteúdo e conferem uma sensação de vida ao site.

Infos

DESIGN: Sven Loskill <www.slad.de> and Emjot <www.emjot.de>. // PROGRAMMING: Emjot. /// TOOLS: Macromedia Flash, xml, php, MySQL. /// COST: Design and Concept: 56 hours. Flash Development: 98 hours. Content Management System Development: 120 hours. /// MAINTENANCE: since we have a customized backend solution to implement our pictures, it depends on the amount of new content to be put online. One new picture takes about a minute. That includes uploading, downsampling and positioning.

ANNA MOLLER PHOTOGRAPHY

www.annamoller.net

Concept

Una sensación de sencillez e intimidad complementa el carácter de las fotografías. //// *Una sensazione di semplicità e d'intimità che rende omaggio al tono delle fotografie.* //// **Uma sensação de simplicidade e intimidade, que complementa o ambiente das fotografias.**

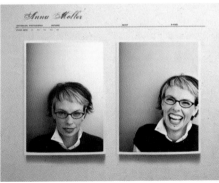

Infos

DESIGN AND PROGRAMMING: Bela Spohrer (ProTrigga Design) <www.protrigga.com>. /// TOOLS: Macromedia Flash. /// COST: 40 hours. /// MAINTENANCE: 1 hour per month.

www.antonwatts.com

Concept

Navegación concisa y grafismo austero. //// Navigazione sintetica e impressione grafica netta. //// Navegação concisa e gráficos claros.

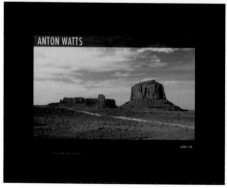

Infos

DESIGN: Chris Christodoulou (Saddington & Baynes) <www.sb-showcase.com>. /// **PROGRAMMING:** Duncan Hart. ///
TOOLS: Adobe Photoshop, Macromedia Flash. /// **COST:** £3,000.

ANTTI VIITALA PHOTO

www.anttiviitala.com

Concept

Ofrecemos al cliente potencial la posibilidad de ver las fotografías con comodidad y sin distracciones. //// Diamo al potenziale cliente la possibilità di vedere le fotografie con facilità e senza distrazioni. //// Damos ao potencial cliente a hipótese de ver as fotografias de uma forma acessível e sem quaisquer distracções.

Infos

DESIGN: Saddington & Baynes <www.sb-showcase.com>. /// TOOLS: Macromedia Flash. /// COST: 1 month. /// MAINTENANCE: 1 hour per month.

BOOGIE PHOTOGRAPHER

USA
2002

www.artcoup.com

Concept

Presenta tanto las fotografías permanentes como las que se añaden a diario de forma totalmente automatizada. //// Il portfolio presenta i post e gli elementi del sito in una struttura di navigazione facile e in modo completamente automatico. //// Apresenta reportagens fotográficas e imagens diárias numa navegação muito fácil de usar, totalmente automática.

Infos

DESIGN: Dead By Design <www.deadbydesign.us>. /// PROGRAMMING: Rastko Samurovic <www.reakcija.com>. /// TOOLS: Macromedia Flash, xml, asp, database. /// COST: 150 hours. /// MAINTENANCE: 5 hours per month.

Concept

La simplicidad y la claridad de una imagen pueden hacer que las cosas luzcan más. //// *La semplicità e la chiarezza di un'immagine possono far apparire migliori le cose.* //// A pureza e a simplicidade de uma imagem podem fazer com que as coisas se apresentem da melhor forma.

Infos

DESIGN: Arturo Esparza (AR2Design). /// **AWARDS:** TINY, e-Creative, DOPE. /// **TOOLS:** html, Action Script, Macromedia Flash, Adobe Photoshop. /// **CONTENT:** music from TYCHO (The Science of Patterns EP), and some images from my portfolio. /// **COST:** 60 hours. /// **MAINTENANCE:** 5 hours per month.

Concept

Arrastre y póngales la cabeza a los robots para activarlos… //// Trascinate la testa per attivare i robot… //// Puxe a cabeça para o sítio pretendido de forma a activar os robôs…

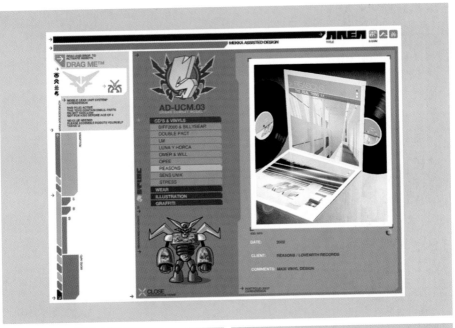

Infos

DESIGN: Alberto Russo and Pascal Wicht (AREADESIGN). /// **PROGRAMMING:** Luigi Iannitelli. /// **AWARDS:** FWA, Moluv's Picks, Bombshock, Golden Web Award. /// **TOOLS:** action script, html, Macromedia Flash, music. /// **COST:** 1 month.

ARJAN VERSCHOOR

www.arjanverschoor.nl

Concept

Un sitio web espacial y personalizado que contiene muchas imágenes y resulta fácil de manejar. //// È un sito costruito nello spazio e per l'utente: gestisce molte immagini ed è facile da manovrare. //// Um site espacial que lida com muitas imagens e é muito fácil de utilizar.

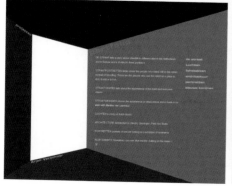

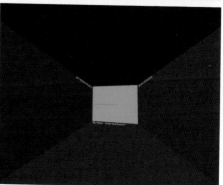

Infos

DESIGN: Gruppen Grafische Vormgeving <www.henkgruppen.nl>. /// **PROGRAMMING:** Henk Gruppen. /// **TOOLS:** Macromedia Flash. /// **COST:** 30 hours. /// **MAINTENANCE:** 2 hours per month.

Concept

Una mirada a una moda llena de color. //// Fashion con colore. //// Forma colorida de encarar a moda.

Infos

DESIGN AND PROGRAMMING: Are Bu Vindenes <www.arervindenes.com>. /// **TOOLS:** Macromedia Flash, html. ///
COST: 50 hours. /// **MAINTENANCE:** 1 hour per month.

ASMALLPERCENT

www.asmallpercent.com

Concept

Facilidad de uso y simplicidad práctica. //// Di facile utilizzo – semplicità funzionale. //// Fácil de usar – simplicidade utilitária.

 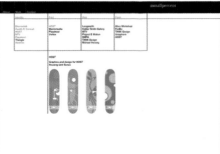

Infos

DESIGN AND PROGRAMMING: Tim Ferguson Sauder (Asmallpercent). /// **TOOLS:** html, Macromedia Flash. /// **COST:** 20 hours. /// **MAINTENANCE:** 1 hour per month.

BEPOSITIVE DESIGN

THAILAND/USA
2001

www.bepositivedesign.com

Concept

La web es como un plato vacío que se llena de sabrosos alimentos. //// Il sito funziona da piatto di portata vuoto da riempire con cibo dai colori vivaci. //// Este site funciona como um prato vazio à espera de ser enchido com comida colorida.

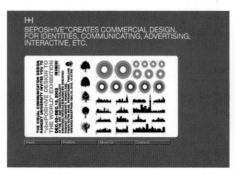 

Infos

DESIGN: Tnop and Bepositive Design. /// **PROGRAMMING:** Akwit Vongsa-ngiam and Tnop Wangsillapakun. /// **TOOLS:** html, Macromedia Flash, dhtml. /// **COST:** 200 hours. /// **MAINTENANCE:** 0-5 hours per month.

Concept

Una típica situación cliente-fotógrafo. //// Una tipica situazione cliente – fotografo. //// Uma típica situação cliente – fotógrafo.

Layout

DESIGN: 52NORD Designbuero <www.52nord.de>. /// **PROGRAMMING:** Sven Stüber. /// **AWARDS:** FWA, e-Creative. /// **TOOLS:** html, Macromedia Flash, music, screenfonts. /// **COST:** 40 hours. /// **MAINTENANCE:** 8 hours every 6 months.

BLUEMAN

www.blueman.com.br

Concept

Moderna, acorde con la identidad visual de la marca. //// Moderno, in linea con l'identità visiva della marca. //// Moderno, consentâneo com a identidade visual da marca.

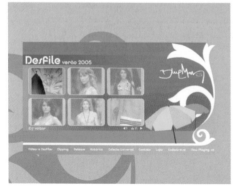

Infos

DESIGN: ZonaInternet <www.zonainternet.com>. /// PROGRAMMING: André Tenenbaum (ZonaInternet). /// TOOLS: html, Macromedia Flash, action-script, xml, asp, music, film. /// COST: 45 days. /// MAINTENANCE: 10 hours per month.

BORIS POLJICANIN PHOTO

www.borispoljicanin.com

Concept

La idea básica consiste en presentar las obsesiones constantes de todo fotógrafo (la luz y la sombra, lo nítido y lo borroso) mediante la incorporación de esos elementos a los contenidos y la navegación de la web. //// *L'idea del sito è quella di presentare le eterne ossessioni dei fotografi, chiaro e scuro, nitido e sfocato, implementando gli elementi nei contenuti e nella navigazione del sito.* //// **A ideia é apresentar, mais concretamente, as eternas obsessões do fotógrafo: luz/escuridão e nitidez/desfocagem, implementando os elementos no conteúdo do site e na navegação.**

Infos

DESIGN AND PROGRAMMING: Igor Skunca (Invent: Multimedia Studio) <www.invent.hr>. /// AWARDS: Croatian Advertising Festival, Magdalena International Advertising Festival of Creative Communications. /// TOOLS: Macromedia Flash, Macromedia Dreamweaver, Adobe Photoshop. /// COST: 100 hours. /// MAINTENANCE: 4 hours per month.

BOXER

www.boxer.uk.com

Concept

Diseñada ante todo para reflejar nuestra personalidad e identidad. Todas las imágenes muestran situaciones cotidianas con un toque especial.

//// Progettato soprattutto per rispecchiare la nostra identità e la personalità. Tutte le immagini mostrano situazioni quotidiane con bizzarri imprevisti.

//// Concebido, antes de mais, para reflectir a nossa personalidade e identidade. Todas as imagens mostram situações do dia-a-dia com peculiaridades subtis.

Infos

DESIGN: Boxer in conjunction with EngageStudio <www.engagestudio.com>. /// PROGRAMMING: James Stone (EngageStudio). /// TOOLS: Macromedia Flash, html. /// COST: £10-15k. /// MAINTENANCE: 2-3 days per month.

Concept

Una web minimalista, clara y fácil de usar, una herramienta atractiva para iluminar las fotografías y los diseños gráficos. ////
Un sito web minimalista, chiaro e facile da usare: uno strumento attraente che intende mettere in luce la fotografia e il lavoro di graphic design. ////
Um site minimalista, claro e fácil de usar como meio atraente que visa centrar a atenção na fotografia e nos trabalhos de design gráfico.

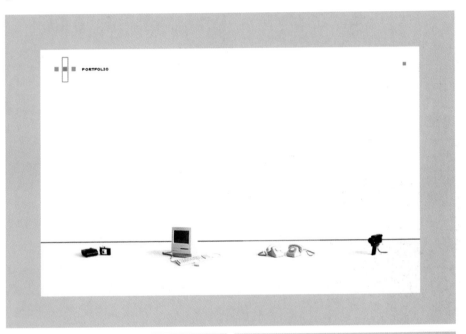

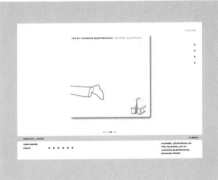

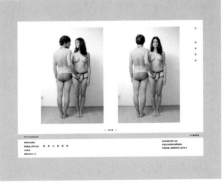

Infos

DESIGN AND PROGRAMMING: Ben Wittner. /// TOOLS: Macromedia Flash, html, Quicktime. /// COST: uncounted number of hours. ///
MAINTENANCE: depending on the works to update.

CALIBREPICS

www.calibrepics.com

Concept

La idea es «llevar las ideas a la práctica». De ahí que se empleara como sistema de navegación un rotulador con el que el visitante subraya adónde quiere ir. //// L'idea è trasformare le idee in realtà. Perciò, come via d'accesso alla navigazione, si usa un disegno in cui gli utenti annotano dove desiderano andare. //// O conceito consiste em transformar as ideias em realidade. Por conseguinte, optou-se por uma navegação que se baseou no acto de desenhar e em que os utilizadores marcam o sítio aonde pretendem aceder.

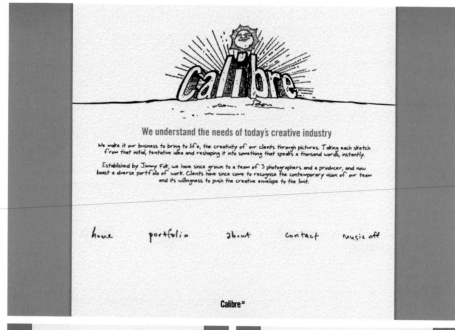

Infos

DESIGN: Kinetic Interactive <www.kinetic.com.sg>. /// PROGRAMMING: Benjy Choo. /// TOOLS: html, Macromedia Flash, php. /// COST: 80 hours. /// MAINTENANCE: 8 hours a week.

CARL DE KEYZER PHOTO

BELGIUM
2004

www.carldekeyzer.com

Concept

Los proyectos que aparecen en el menú se deslizan tras un panel que muestra la vista previa y una breve descripción de cada uno de ellos. ////
I progetti elencati nelle pagine di menù scorrono al di sotto di un magnifico pannello su cui appare un'anteprima e una breve descrizione di ogni progetto.
La pagina del menù scompare quando si seleziona un progetto in modo da poter presentare tutti i titoli sul display. //// Os projectos enumerados nas
páginas do menu desenrolam-se por detrás de um painel magnífico que apresenta um resumo e uma descrição breve de cada projecto.

Infos

DESIGN AND PROGRAMMING: group94 <www.group94.com>. /// AWARDS: Bombshock, BestFlashAnimationSite.com, FWA (Site of the Day/Site of the Month),
Netdiver Design Forte, Flash Kit (Site of the Week). /// TOOLS: Macromedia Flash, php, MySQL. /// COST: 7 weeks.

CAROL ACORD PHOTOGRAPHY

USA
2003

www.carolacord.com

Concept

Tras contemplar los trabajos de Carol, supimos de inmediato que las mismas fotografías debían llevar la voz cantante. //// Dopo aver visionato il
corpus delle opere di Carol, siamo stati subito consapevoli che la stessa fotografia avrebbe dovuto avere la voce più potente. //// Após contemplar o
trabalho de Carola Cord, percebemos imediatamente que a fotografia deve estar no centro das atenções.

Infos

DESIGN: Struck Design <www.struckdesign.com>. /// PROGRAMMING: Ryan Goodwin. /// AWARDS: FWA, TINY (Site of the Week), HOW Magazine Interactive
Annual, AIGA 100. /// TOOLS: Macromedia Flash, html, Adobe AfterEffects. /// COST: 35 hours. /// MAINTENANCE: very few.

COLIN GORDON

www.chimpchum.freeserve.co.uk

Concept

Esta web se diseñó para que fuera sencilla y de navegación fácil, se cargara con rapidez y no aparecieran molestas ventanas emergentes. ////
Il sito è stato progettato per essere semplice e di facile navigazione, veloce da caricare e senza pop-up che distraggono l'attenzione. //// O site foi
concebido para ser simples e fácil de navegar, rápido a carregar e sem pop-ups que distraiam.

Infos

DESIGN AND PROGRAMMING: Colin Gordon. /// TOOLS: Adobe Illustrator, Macromedia Dreamweaver. /// COST: 25 hours. /// MAINTENANCE: 2 hours per month.

CLARK STUDIOS

www.clark-studios.com

Concept

La carátula de disco en la página principal y la estantería para CD en el porfolio constituían la manera perfecta de «casar» nuestra pasión por la música y el diseño. //// L'home page con le etichette di dischi da collezione e la navigazione all'interno dei portfolio a forma di CD era il modo perfetto per "coniugare" la nostra passione per la musica e per il design. //// A página com a capa de um disco antigo e a navegação com os portfólios em caixas de CD foi a forma ideal para combinar a nossa paixão pela música e pelo design.

Infos

DESIGN AND PROGRAMMING: Justin Clark (Clark Studios). /// TOOLS: html, Macromedia Flash, digital camera. Sound mixed by Rick Truhls. /// COST: 60 hours. /// MAINTENANCE: 4 hours per month.

COLOPLAY STUDIO

www.coloplay.hu

Concept

El concepto no tenía que incluir palabras: dejamos que nuestros trabajos hablen por sí solos. //// L'idea era non usare parole e lasciare che i lavori presentati parlassero da soli. //// A ideia consistiu em não ter palavras e deixar que os trabalhos falem por si.

Infos

DESIGN: Gábor Balogh [ColoPLAY]. /// **PROGRAMMING:** Péter Nehoda [ColoPLAY]. /// **AWARDS:** Hungarian Webdesign [Site of the Week]. /// **TOOLS:** Macromedia Flash, php, Adobe Photoshop, Adobe Illustrator. /// **COST:** 90 hours. /// **MAINTENANCE:** 5-8 hours per month.

DANYBOY.COM

www.danyboy.com

Concept

Web personal de graffiti. ¡Rompe el huevo de dinosaurio y entra! //// Un sito personale di graffiti: rompete l'uovo di dinosauro per scoprirlo! //// Site de graffiti pessoal. Vamos partir o ovo do dinossauro para ficarmos a saber mais!

Infos

DESIGN: Danyboy <www.danyboy.com>; <www.semperultimo.com>. /// **PROGRAMMING:** 16ar <www.16argarden.com>; Gus <www.semperultimo.com>. /// **AWARDS:** FWA. /// **TOOLS:** Macromedia Flash, D'n'B music. /// **COST:** 300 hours. /// **MAINTENANCE:** every month.

Concept

En esta versión el concepto era mucho más profundo e interior, y por eso recurrí a una gama de tonos oscuros, una tipografía angustiosa y un sonido inquietante. //// È una versione con un concept interno molto più profondo, caratterizzato da gamme cromatiche scure, un carattere tipografico e un sonoro angoscioso. //// Esta versão necessitou de uma conceptualização interna mais elaborada, com a paleta de cores escuras, a tipografia angustiante e o som.

Infos

DESIGN: D5ive. /// **PROGRAMMING:** Paul B. Drohan and Chris Andrade. /// **AWARDS:** Flash Forward & Film Festival, STEP Inside magazine. /// **TOOLS:** Macromedia Flash, Adobe Photoshop, Macromedia Freehand. /// **COST:** 40-50 hours.

Concept

La página principal se creó a partir de una obra escaneada hecha de plástico, silicona, pintura aerosol gris y materiales de desecho. Fue elegida por su sencillez. //// La pagina iniziale è costruita partendo dalla scansione di un'opera d'arte realizzata in plastica, silicone, vernice spray di colore grigio e materiale di recupero scelto per le sue linee semplici. //// A página principal foi concebida a partir de uma obra de arte feita de plástico, silicone, tinta de spray cinzenta e materiais encontrados, escolhidos pelo seu design simples.

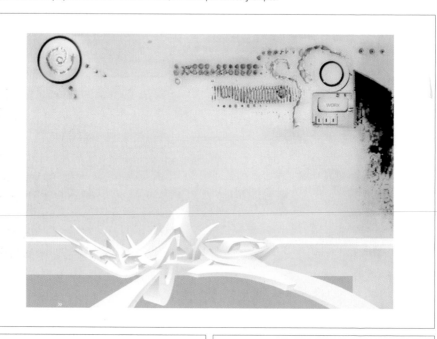

Infos

DESIGN AND PROGRAMMING: Sascha Thoma (Delcasto.de). /// TOOLS: Macromedia Flash, html, Quicktime. /// COST: 5 months. /// MAINTENANCE: depends on the freetime.

DETREMMERIE

www.detremmerie.be

Concept

Por esta web se navega con rapidez y sin ningún «espere mientras se carga», ya que todas las imágenes se cargan previamente y por lo tanto sólo son accesibles cuando ya están disponibles. //// Il sito ha una navigazione veloce e senza attese di caricamento, poiché tutte le immagini dispongono di un preload e sono dunque accessibili solo quando sono state effettivamente caricate. //// O site navega de forma rápida e sem quaisquer indicações de "espere enquanto carrega", na medida em que todas as imagens já estão pré-carregadas e, deste modo, apenas acessíveis quando são realmente carregadas.

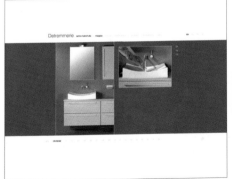

Infos

DESIGN AND PROGRAMMING: group94 <www.group94.com>. /// AWARDS: FWA (Site of the Day). /// TOOLS: Macromedia Flash, php, MySQL. /// COST: 5 weeks. /// MAINTENANCE: 1-2 days every 6 months.

Concept

Lo que de hecho se visita es mi disco duro, donde guardo todos mis trabajos. //// In realtà, è una visita all'hard disk in cui archivio il mio lavoro. //// Na verdade, está a visitar o meu disco rígido em que o meu trabalho está arquivado.

RELOAD 25 / 2004
I WAS GIVEN THE EDITORIAL PAGE TO BOMB. SO I DID. (IT'S A JUNGLE OUT THERE)

Infos

DESIGN: Hugo Mulder (DHM). /// PROGRAMMING: Rogier Mulder. /// TOOLS: Macromedia Flash, music. /// COST: too much, I can't remenber. /// MAINTENANCE: 10 hours per month.

DHP ARCHITECTEN

www.dhp-architecten.be

Concept

Sencilla, austera, dinámica, sorprendente... Explórela. //// Semplice, chiaro, dinamico, sorprendente: da esplorare... //// Simples, puro, dinâmico, surpreendente, a explorar...

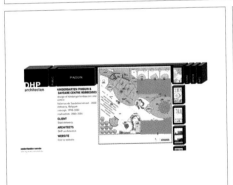

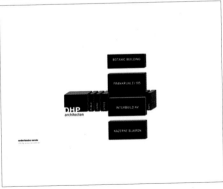

Infos

DESIGN: pieter Lesage and Ann Bruyns (Concrete) <www.concrete.be>. /// PROGRAMMING: Onno Baudouin (Concrete). /// AWARDS: Netdiver, flashmxpro.com, DOPE, Moluv's Picks, crossmind.net, netinspiration.com, digitalthread.com, thedreamer.com.br, nicewebsite.co.uk, etc. /// TOOLS: Macromedia Flash, xml. /// COST: 150 hours. /// MAINTENANCE: a few hours per month.

DIRK HOFFMANN

www.dirkhoffmann.net

GERMANY
2004

Concept
Dibujos insólitos en una interfaz minimalista. //// Disegni insoliti con un'interfaccia minimalista. //// Desenhos pouco comuns num interface minimalista.

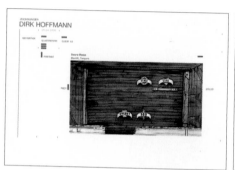

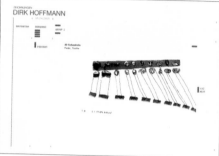

Infos
DESIGN: Dirk Hoffmann and Patrik de Jong <www.punktx.com>. /// **PROGRAMMING:** Patrik de Jong. /// **AWARDS:** TINY (featured site - Categorie Art). /// **TOOLS:** Macromedia Flash. /// **COST:** 260 hours. /// **MAINTENANCE:** 4 hours per month.

DIRK LAMBRECHTS PHOTO

www.dirklambrechts.com

BELGIUM
2003

Concept
La idea era crear un ambiente técnico, de caja de luz, con un sistema de navegación de lo más intuitivo: se pincha para abrir la imagen, para ampliarla, para reducirla. //// Il concept di base era creare un'atmosfera tecnica da "lightbox" con un sistema di navigazione molto intuitivo: un click per aprire, un click per ingrandire, un click per ridimensionare. //// Pretendemos criar um ambiente técnico "parecido com uma caixa" com um sistema de navegação muito intuitivo: click para abrir, click para alargar, click para reduzir.

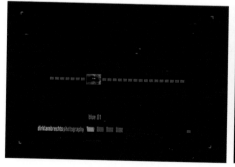

Infos
DESIGN AND PROGRAMMING: Group94 <www.group94.com> /// **AWARDS:** FWA (Site of the Day). /// **TOOLS:** Macromedia Flash. /// **COST:** 4 weeks. /// **MAINTENANCE:** 1 day every 6 months.

STEVE DOUBLE PHOTOGRAPHY

USA
1999

www.double-whammy.com

Concept

El diseño se deja en segundo plano para que toda la atención se centre en las fotografías, y se entretiene al usuario con una divertida interfaz de navegación. //// Ha un design dai toni smorzati per permettere di soffermare l'attenzione sulle fotografie e un'interfaccia di navigazione divertente per attrarre l'utente. //// Um design atenuado para permitir que a atenção incida sobre as fotografias e com uma navegação divertida para atrair o visitante.

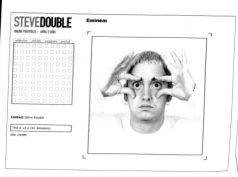

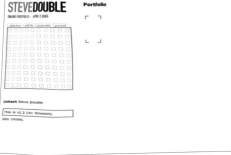

Infos

DESIGN AND PROGRAMMING: Angus Keith <www.adaadat.com>. /// AWARDS: Net Design (Best Site), Max Hits: Building and Promoting Successful Websites. /// TOOLS: dhtml, Javascript, Textpad, Adobe Photoshop, Adobe Illustrator, asp, MySQL. /// COST: 120 hours. /// MAINTENANCE: 5 hours per month.

DREAM INTERACTIVE

HUNGARY
2005

www.dream.hu

Concept

La web actual se creó como una página provisional donde presentar brevemente algunos de nuestros trabajos más recientes y nuestra dedicación al diseño profesional. //// Il sito attuale è stato creato in via provvisoria per presentare brevemente alcune delle nostre ultime creazioni e la dedizione al design professionale. //// Este site foi criado temporariamente com o objectivo de apresentar brevemente alguns dos nossos trabalhos actuais e a nossa dedicação ao design profissional.

Infos

DESIGN: Gábor Tuba, Zsolt Vajda (Dream Interactive) <www.dream.hu>. /// PROGRAMMING: Tamás Turcsányi, Gábor Nagy (Dream Interactive) /// TOOLS: html, CSS, Macromedia Flash, xml, php, Smarty. /// COST: 25-30 hours. /// MAINTENANCE: 6-8 hours per month.

DOUGLAS FISHER PHOTOGRAPHY   UK

www.douglasfisher.co.uk   2004

Concept

Porfolio con un sistema de navegación fluido. El tipo de material que contiene requería que los minimalistas y «sencillos» elementos gráficos se centraran al máximo en las imágenes. //// Portfolio caratterizzato da un fluido sistema di navigazione. Il tipo di immagini ha richiesto degli elementi grafici minimalisti e "semplici" in modo da potersi concentrare il più possibile sulle immagini in sé. //// Portfólio com um sistema de navegação fluido. Recorre a um tipo de imagens apropriado a elementos gráficos minimalistas e "simples", de forma a centrar-se o mais possível nas próprias imagens.

Infos

DESIGN AND PROGRAMMING: Group94 <www.group94.com> /// TOOLS: Macromedia Flash, php. /// COST: 6 weeks.

Concept

DiSeñar es como rizar un rizo en infinita evolución! //// DeSign è un loop che si evolve all'infinito! //// DeSign é um looping em evolução para a eternidade!

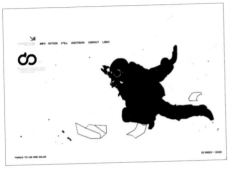 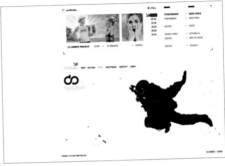

Infos

DESIGN: Everson Nazari (DSLAB). /// **PROGRAMMING:** Fábio Oliveira. /// **TOOLS:** html, Macromedia Flash, asp, movie, illustration, web, identity. /// **COST:** 40-60 hours. /// **MAINTENANCE:** 20 hours per month.

EL GRANDO BEAUTY SALON

ESTONIA
2004

www.elgrando.ee

Concept

Impresionante y a la vez muy informativa. Con clase. //// Di grande effetto ma ricco d'informazioni e di glamour. //// Impressionante, muito informativo e glamoroso.

Infos

DESIGN: Vladimir Morozov (Lime Creative) <www.lime.ee>. /// **PROGRAMMING:** Sander Sellin, Vladimir Morozov. /// **AWARDS:** FWA (Site of the day). /// **TOOLS:** Macromedia Flash, html, php. /// **COST:** 250 hours. /// **MAINTENANCE:** 5 hours per month.

DUNUN

www.dunun.com

Concept

El mundo de Dunun es tan coherente como el nuestro. En él puede verse (desde la ventana y en tiempo real) cómo los sonidos y el paisaje de navegación cambian con el paso del tiempo. //// Dunun è un mondo coerente come il nostro. Vedrete (quasi come se foste affacciati alla finestra e in contemporanea) cambiare con il tempo l'ambiente sonoro e lo scenario di navigazione. //// O Dunun é um mundo consistente, tal como o vosso. Terá a oportunidade de ver (quase como se fosse a partir da sua própria janela e durante os mesmos momentos) o tempo a alterar o ambiente sonoro e a paisagem de navegação.

Infos

DESIGN: Dunun. /// PROGRAMMING: Micael Reynaud. /// AWARDS: FWA, Bombshock, TINY, fcukstar.com, wellvetted.com, Plasticpilots, Flash Forward, Flashxpress, Designfirms.org, Flash In The Can.com. /// TOOLS: Macromedia Flash, xml, php, html, JavaScript. /// CONTENT: interactive music, photo, video. /// COST: 500 hours. /// MAINTENANCE: 50 hours per month.

SACHA DEAN BIYAN

www.eccentris.com

Concept

Vanguardista fotografía de moda, diseño web, música y animación se fusionan para crear una experiencia sensorial única. Sacha Biyan imaginaba una web «a la última» en todos los sentidos. ///// Il sito fonde fotografía di moda e all'avanguardia, web design, musica e animazione per creare un'esperienza sensoriale unica. Sacha Biyan lo ha immaginato "d'alto valore" in ogni aspetto. ///// Uma fusão de fotografía de moda vanguardista com web design, música e movimento, de forma a criar uma experiência sensorial única. Sacha Biyan quis que o seu site se caracterizasse pela alta qualidade em todos os aspectos.

Infos

DESIGN: Rita Lidji (Firstborn) <www.firstbornmultimedia.com>. /// PROGRAMMING: Josh Ott. /// AWARDS: Communication Arts, Flash In The Can, FWA. /// TOOLS: Macromedia Flash, SoundForge, Adobe AfterEffects, Adobe Premiere. /// COST: 400 hours.

MONICA CALVO

www.eendar.com

Concept

Eendar.com se creó a partir de los colores de una antigua pintura japonesa. Quería algo que fuera muy sencillo y agradable a la vista, y con un sistema de navegación simple. //// Eendar.com è nato basandosi sui colori di un antico dipinto giapponese. Ho scelto qualcosa di semplice e carino alla vista e che permetta una navigazione semplice. //// Eendar.com foi criado com base nas cores de uma pintura japonesa antiga. Quis criar algo muito simples, agradável de ver e com uma navegação fácil.

copyright mónica calvo 2003/2004
www.organicfields.net

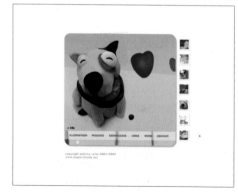

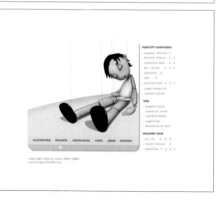

Infos

DESIGN: Monica Calvo. /// PROGRAMMING: Monica Calvo and Carlos Rincon. /// TOOLS: Adobe Photoshop, html, Macromedia Flash. /// COST: 32 hours. /// MAINTENANCE: 2 hours per month.

ESAO.NET

www.esao.net

Concept

Una web interactiva donde se exponen las pinturas del artista y otros trabajos. El diseño de la web es una extensión de su obra más que una mera presentación. //// Un sito web interattivo: mostra i quadri dell'artista e altre opere in un design che non si limita a presentare la sua arte ma ne costituisce un prolungamento. //// Um site interactivo que expõe as pinturas e outros trabalhos do artista, sendo o design actual uma extensão da sua arte e não apenas uma forma de a apresentar.

Infos

DESIGN AND PROGRAMMING: Esao Andrews. /// TOOLS: Macromedia Flash. /// COST: worked on during spare time. /// MAINTENANCE: $15.00 per month via <www.crystaltech.com>.

FARUK AKIN PROJECT

www.farukakin.com

Concept

El concepto del diseño viene a ser algo así como la caseta de tiro al blanco de una feria. Es una página interactiva que contiene obras en 2D y en 3D; para verlas, sólo hay que mover el cursor a la derecha o a la izquierda. //// Il concetto di design, che assomiglia ad un gioco di tiro, è un parco. La pagina interattiva mostra i lavori sia in 2D sia 3D, basta semplicemente scrollare a destra o a sinistra. //// O conceito do design recorda os jogos de tiro ao alvo nas feiras populares. A página interactiva apresenta trabalhos em 2D e 3D, bastando mexer o rato para a direita ou para a esquerda.

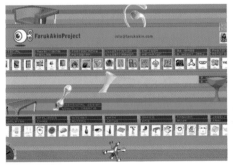
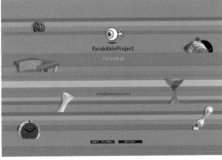

Infos

DESIGN: Faruk Akin Project <www.farukakin.com>. /// PROGRAMMING: Guven Dinneden. /// TOOLS: Macromedia Flash.

www.emmanuellebernard.com

Concept

Austera y femenina. Las fotos son la máxima prioridad de la web. //// Lineare e femminile. Le fotografie sono la priorità principale del sito. //// Feminino e puro. As fotografias constituem a maior prioridade deste site.

Infos

DESIGN: Bruno Fraga (6D estúdio) <www.6d.com.br>. /// PROGRAMMING: Gabriel Marques (6D estúdio). /// TOOLS: Macromedia Flash. /// COST: 320 hours. /// MAINTENANCE: 8 hours per month.

Concept

Tratamos de destacar los trabajos de la mejor manera posible exponiéndolos en una web atractiva y de gran calidad técnica desarrollada con Flash. //// Abbiamo cercato di mettere in luce il lavoro nel miglior modo possibile, mostrandolo in un sito web d'alto valore tecnico realizzato con Flash che colpisce l'attenzione. //// Tentámos destacar o trabalho da melhor maneira possível, ao mesmo tempo que o expomos num site em Flash de alta qualidade e visualmente cativante.

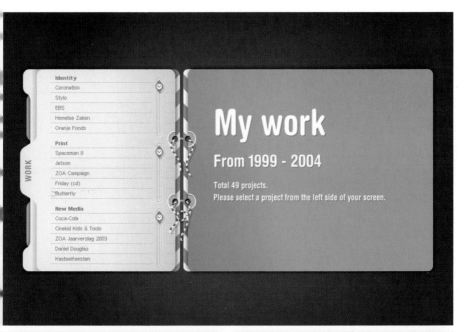

Infos

DESIGN: Erik Otten. /// **PROGRAMMING:** Seraph (www.seraph.nl). /// **AWARDS:** FWA, TINY (Site of the Month), Netdiver, fcukstar.com, Kirupa. /// **TOOLS:** Macromedia Fireworks, Adobe Illustrator, Macromedia Flash. /// **COST:** 200 hours. /// **MAINTENANCE:** 1 hour per month.

www.estherfranklin.co.uk

Concept

Las influencias de la web: estados de ánimo nocturnos y una elegancia inteligente y sexy. //// Influenze del sito: dalle atmosfere notturne all'eleganza disinvolta e sensuale. //// Influências do site: ambientes nocturnos com elegância pura e sexy.

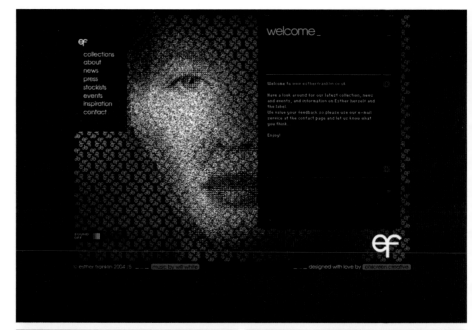

Infos

DESIGN: Onscreen Creative <www.onscreencreative.com>. /// **PROGRAMMING:** Rob and Zulma. /// **MUSIC:** Will White. /// **TOOLS:** Adobe Photoshop, Adobe Illustrator, Macromedia Flash, Macromedia Dreamweaver, php. /// **COST:** 6-8 weeks.

Concept

Exactitudes.com visualiza la compleja relación entre el individuo y el grupo: la aparente contradicción entre desear desmarcarse de los demás y ser único y asumir una identidad colectiva. //// Exactitudes.com visualizza la relazione complessa tra l'individualità e la collettività: la contraddizione apparente tra desiderio d'isolamento e d'identità di gruppo. //// O exactitudes.com visualiza a relação complexa entre a individualidade e a colectividade: a contradição aparente entre o desejo de sobressair dos restantes e ser único e assumir uma identidade de grupo.

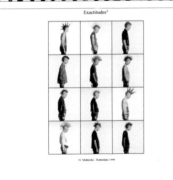

Exactitudes®

24. Mohawks - Rotterdam 1998

Exactitudes®

61. Sunflolor - Rio de Janeiro 2000

Infost

DESIGN: Ari Versluis, Ellie Uyttenbroek and Joost Burger <www.i-b-o-o.com>. /// PROGRAMMING: Joost Burger. /// TOOLS: php, html. /// COST: 4 days. /// MAINTENANCE: 3 hours per month.

FABIAAN VAN SEVEREN

www.fabiaanvanseveren.com

Concept

Un porfolio minimalista con un inteligente sistema de carga. El contenido se puede llevar y traer, como si se estuvieran abriendo y cerrando los cajones de un armario. //// È un portfolio minimalista dal caricamento intelligente in cui i contenuti possono essere tirati fuori e rimessi via, come i cassetti di un armadio che si aprono e si chiudono. //// Um portfólio minimalista, que se carrega de forma inteligente, em que o conteúdo pode ser retirado e afastado, como se se tratasse de uma gaveta que se pode abrir e fechar.

FabiaanVanSeveren | MAY 17

01 CHAIRS
02 TABLES
03 CUPBOARDS
04 LIGHTING
05 BEDS
06 BAGS
07 SPECIALS

PDF CATALOGUE

NEWS | CREW | PROJECTS | SHOWROOM | CONTACT

Infos

DESIGN AND PROGRAMMING: MMM (Multimediamadness) <www.multimediamadness.be>. /// AWARDS: FWA. /// TOOLS: html, xml, Macromedia Flash, php, MySQL. /// COST: 150 hours. /// MAINTENANCE: 1/2 hour per month. Thanks to an excellent CMS.

FLATLINER

www.flatlineronline.com

Concept

Estilo acorde al de las ilustraciones que expone: sencillo, austero y gráfico. Interfaz y navegación suponen una traslación sencilla de lo que serían las distintas pestañas de un porfolio impreso. //// Progettato per riprodurre lo stile delle illustrazioni che si trovano in mostra al momento, dalle semplici linee grafiche. La navigazione e l'esposizione rappresentano un'approssimazione delle copertine dei portfolio a stampa. //// Concebido para ter um estilo semelhante às ilustrações actuais que expõe, ou seja, simples e gráfico. Navegação e apresentação representam uma abordagem simples às capas de um portfólio impresso.

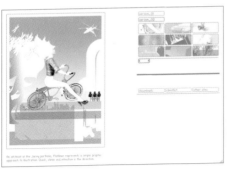
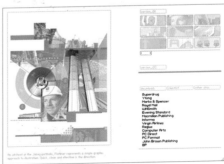

Infos

DESIGN AND PROGRAMMING: Jason Cook <www.jasoncook.co.uk>. /// TOOLS: Macromedia Flash, html. /// COST: 12 hours. /// MAINTENANCE: updated once every 3 months.

FOSOD STUDIOS

www.fosod.com

Concept

Perseguimos incansables tres ideales: simplicidad, facilidad de uso y elegancia. //// Abbiamo costantemente incoraggiato tre idee: semplicità, facilità d'utilizzo ed eleganza. //// Esforçámo-nos incessantemente por atingir três objectivos: simplicidade, facilidade de utilização e elegância.

Infos

DESIGN AND PROGRAMMING: Walter T. Stevenson (Fosod Studios). /// AWARDS: Aljapaco, Biomutation, VIPE, CreativePublic (Site of the Month), Design Inspiration, NewWebPick (Very Cool Site), CoolestDesigns, Plasticpilots (One Star) /// TOOLS: xhtml, CSS, Macromedia Flash, xml, MIDI, Mp3, audio editing applications, Mpeg, video editing applications. /// COST: 2 months. /// MAINTENANCE: 5 hours per month maintenance, redesigned annually.

FINGER INDUSTRIES

www.fingerindustries.co.uk

Concept

Creamos un paisaje urbano en el que el menú principal es un poste indicador y cada apartado se encuentra en un edificio distinto. //// Abbiamo sviluppato una città in cui il menu principale è un segnale stradale e ogni area è situata in un diverso edificio. //// Desenvolvemos a paisagem citadina com um sinal de estrada como menu principal e cada uma das áreas localizada no interior de um edifício diferente.

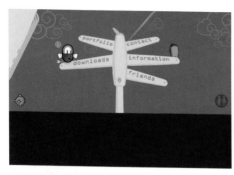 

Infos

DESIGN AND PROGRAMMING: Marcus Kenyon and Jonny Ford (Finger Industries). /// AWARDS: Netdiver Design Forte, American Design Award (Gold), TAXI (Site of the day), NewWebPick. /// TOOLS: Macromedia Flash, Discreet Plasma. /// COST: 6 weeks over 3 months. /// MAINTENANCE: 5 hours per month.

FLORIAN LOHMANN PHOTO

www.florianlohmann.de

Concept

Un apasionado porfolio fotográfico presentado por una chica sexy. //// Un portfolio di fotografia appassionato presentato da una "chica" sexy. //// Um apaixonante portfólio de fotografia apresentado por um "chica" sexy.

Infos

DESIGN: Slick <www.slickdesign.de>. /// PROGRAMMING: Johannes Auffermann. /// TOOLS: Macromedia Flash, video (blue box), xml, html. /// COST: 250 hours. /// MAINTENANCE: 4 hours per month.

Concept

El sistema de navegación de la web es acorde al modo en que Fluid afronta la zona crítica entre entretenimiento y funcionalidad. //// La navigazione del sito si unisce al modo in cui Fluid tratta la zona d'alta tensione tra giocosità e funzionalità. //// A navegação do site relaciona-se com a maneira com que a Fluid lida com a zona de alta tensão entre o elemento lúdico e a funcionalidade.

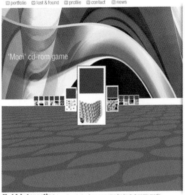

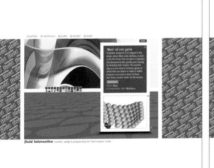
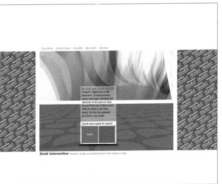

DESIGN AND PROGRAMMING: Remon Tijssen (Fluid). /// **AWARDS:** FWA. /// **TOOLS:** Macromedia Director, Macromedia Flash, html, interactivity, behaviors, animation, video, audio, text. /// **COST:** 2-3 months. /// **MAINTENANCE:** 4 hours per month.

FOR OFFICE USE ONLY

www.forofficeuseonly.com

Concept

La idea: crear una interfaz que pudiera actualizarse y hacer que la estética y el funcionamiento de la web fueran coherentes con el estilo global y las ideas del estudio. //// Il concept: creare un'interfaccia aggiornabile e che rendesse l'estetica e il funzionamento del sito coerente con lo stile e le idee globali dello studio. //// O conceito: criar um interface que possa ser actualizável, e fazer com que a estética e o comportamento do site seja coerente com o estilo e as ideias globais do estúdio.

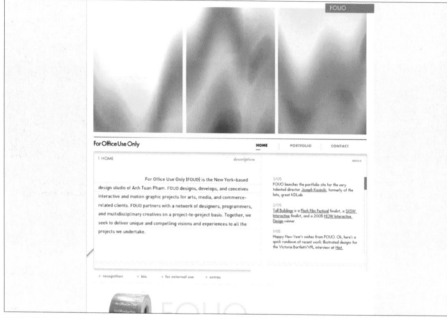

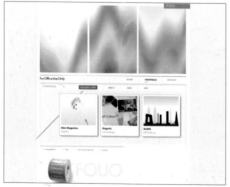

Infos

DESIGN AND PROGRAMMING: For Office Use Only. /// TOOLS: Macromedia Flash, Adobe Photoshop, Adobe Illustrator, SoundEdit.

FU-DESIGN.COM

www.fu-design.com

Concept

Fu-design.com es un lugar creativo y alegre donde se muestran las obras de arte, la música y las animaciones de Chu Keng Fu. //// FU-design.com è un sito creativo e allegro con le opere artistiche di Chu Keng Fu, musica e animazioni. //// A fu-design.com é um sítio criativo e alegre onde poderá encontrar os trabalhos artísticos de Chu Keng Fu, música e animações.

Infos

DESIGN AND PROGRAMMING: Chu Keng Fu (FU-Design). /// AWARDS: Netdiver (BOTY), FWA (Site Of The Day), Plasticpilots (Two Star), TINY, Graphics.com Team, Coolhomepage.com, Coolstop's Portal Cool Zone, Noteworthy Cool Site, Upwardlink. /// TOOLS: Macromedia Flash, Adobe Photoshop, Macromedia Dreamweaver. /// COST: 1 month. /// MAINTENANCE: 1 hour a day.

GIOSIMI

www.giosimi.com

Concept

Si te repites, estás acabado. //// Sei finito se ti ripeti. //// Quando se começa a repetir, está-se acabado.

Infos

DESIGN: Giosimi. /// PROGRAMMING: Giosimi and Zoltan. /// TOOLS: Macromedia Flash, Adobe Illustrator, Lightwave 3D , html. /// COST: 20 hours. /// MAINTENANCE: 4-6 hours per month.

FREAKY FACETS

www.freakyfacets.com

2004

Navegación sencilla para exponer obras personales de ilustración, de las que hacen que la gente se incorpore y pregunte: «¿Quién es este chalado?». //// Una navigazione semplice senza fatica, per mostrare dei lavori personali d'illustrazione che fanno saltare in piedi la gente ed esclamare: "Chi è il più pazzo"? //// Navegação simples e fácil para apresentar alguns trabalhos de ilustração pessoais com o objectivo de fazer as pessoas coçar a cabeça e pensarem "quem é este maluco?".

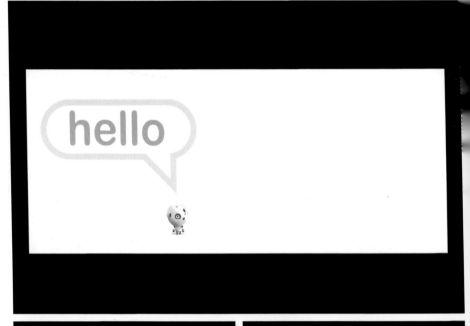

DESIGN AND PROGRAMMING: John Taylor (Freaky Facets). /// **TOOLS:** html, Macromedia Flash, Adobe Illustrator, Adobe Photoshop. /// **COST:** 2 months. /// **MAINTENANCE:** minimal hours per month.

GALLAGHER & ASSOCIATES

www.gallagherdesign.com

Concept

Este porfolio de 4 niveles consiste en un sistema de paneles móviles y cambiantes que muestran la estructura del sitio de un modo intuitivo y visual. //// Questo portfolio a 4 livelli di profondità consiste in un sistema di pannelli galleggianti e pieghevoli, che presentano la struttura in un modo intuitivo e visivo. //// Este portfólio de 4 níveis consiste num sistema de painéis flutuantes e desdobráveis que expõe a estrutura de uma forma intuitiva e visual.

Intro

DESIGN AND PROGRAMMING: group94 <www.group94.com>. /// TOOLS: Macromedia Flash, php, MySQL. /// COST: 5 weeks.

GIGUE FASHION

www.gigue.com

Concept

Aunque consta básicamente de imágenes, no es necesario esperar mientras se cargan, ya que los botones aparecen (y, por lo tanto, se pueden pinchar) cuando la imagen en cuestión ya está cargada. //// Anche se il sito contiene per lo più immagini, non c'è bisogno di attenderne il caricamento poiché ogni bottone si genera da solo e, quindi, è pronto per essere cliccato, nel momento stesso in cui l'immagine richiesta è caricata. //// Apesar de conter sobretudo imagens, não é necessário "esperar carregar". Cada botão é criado, e portanto apto a ser clicado, no momento em que a imagem pretendida está a ser carregada.

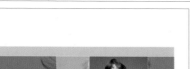

Infos

DESIGN AND PROGRAMMING: Group94 <www.group94.com> /// TOOLS: Macromedia Flash, php. /// COST: 4 weeks. /// MAINTENANCE: 2 days every 6 months.

I AM SIA

SWEDEN
2003

www.iamsia.com

Viejo de verdad, aún no. //// *Antico ma non vecchio.* //// Verdadeiramente antigo sem, no entanto, o chegar a ser.

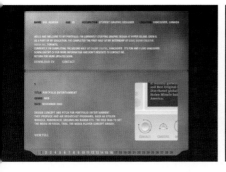 

DESIGN: Sia Ashegh (I Am Sia) <www.iamsia.com>. /// PROGRAMMING: Emmanuel Adams. /// TOOLS: Macromedia Flash, html. /// COST: 8-10 hours /// MAINTENANCE: almost nothing.

GRUPPEN DESIGN

THE NETHERLANDS
2002

www.henkgruppen.nl

La web refleja los principios creativos de GGV: diseños claros, coherentes y sobrios. Lo cual no quiere decir «sencillos». Lograr que un diseño sea claro, coherente y sobrio no es tan sencillo... //// *Il sito riflette i principi di web design del GGV: chiarezza, coerenza e concretezza. Da non confondersi con la semplicità. Creare un design chiaro, coerente e concreto non è per nulla semplice...* //// O site reflecte os princípios de design da GGV: designs claros, consistentes e sóbrios, características que não devem ser confundidas com simplicidade. Manter um design claro, consistente e sóbrio não é assim tão fácil...

DESIGN AND PROGRAMMING: Gruppen Grafische Vormgeving. /// TOOLS: Macromedia Flash. /// COST: 20 hours. /// MAINTENANCE: 1 hour per month.

Concept

Hace un año me mudé de Ciudad de México a Estados Unidos y redescubrí mis raíces. Ése es el motor de h4che: la añoranza de los sabores, colores y sonidos de mi país. //// Un anno fa, mi sono trasferito negli Stati Uniti da Città del Messico e ho riscoperto le mie radici. È stata la spinta creativa di "h4ache": poiché mi mancavano i sapori, i colori e i suoni della mia terra. //// Há um ano mudei-me da Cidade do México para os EUA e redescubri minha raízes. Foi este o sentimento que impulsionou a criação da h4che: as saudades dos aromas, dos sabores, das cores e dos sons do meu país.

Infos

DESIGN AND PROGRAMMING: Jorge Calleja (H4CHE) <www.h4che.com>; <www.l3che.com>. /// **AWARDS:** TAXI, e-Creative, Newstoday, Uialab, Gold Addy, Best in Show. /// **TOOLS:** digital camera, Adobe Photoshop, Macromedia Flash. /// **COST:** 3 months. /// **MAINTENANCE:** 2 hours per month.

HEIMO PHOTOGRAPHY

www.heimophotography.com

Una interfaz para mostrar las fotografías de Heimo de forma entretenida pero sin restar valor a la obra en sí. //// Un'interfaccia per mostrare la fotografia di Heimo in modo divertente e senza distrarre dal lavoro stesso. //// Um interface para expor as fotografias de Heimo de uma forma divertida, sem minimizar o trabalho em si.

DESIGN AND PROGRAMMING: Andreas Tagger, Butler, Shine, Stern and Partners <www.projectangora.com>, <www.bsands.com>. /// AWARDS: One Show (Silver Pencil). /// TOOLS: Adobe Photoshop, Adobe Illustrator, Macromedia Flash, BBEdit. /// COST: 100 hours. /// MAINTENANCE: 1 hour per month.

HELLO DESIGN

www.hellodesign.com

Concept

Creemos en la construcción de sistemas útiles, usables y deseables. //// Il concept di partenza è rispecchiare l'idea che Hello Design crea sistemi intelligenti e vivibili da sperimentare. Crediamo nella costruzione di sistemi utili, utilizzabili e desiderabili. //// Acreditamos na construção de sistemas úteis, utilizáveis e apetecíveis.

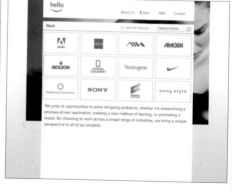

Infos

DESIGN: David Lai, Hiro Niwa, Christel Leung, Szu Ann Chen and George Lee (Hello Design). /// **PROGRAMMING:** Dan Phiffer. /// **TOOLS:** Macromedia Flash, html, xml, MySQL. /// **COST:** 3 months.

HIDDEN BROOK STUDIO

USA

www.hiddenbrookstudio.com

2004

Nuestro objetivo era mostrar el entorno en el que vive y trabaja la fotógrafa: los sonidos de la naturaleza y de los animales, el clima, el ambiente.
//// Il nostro scopo è illustrare l'ambiente in cui il fotografo vive e lavora, i suoni della natura e degli animali, il passaggio delle stagioni, l'atmosfera. ////
O nosso objectivo consistiu em ilustrar o ambiente em que o fotógrafo vive e trabalha, os sons da natureza e dos animais, a temperatura sazonal,
o ambiente.

Infos

DESIGN: Giorgio Baravalle (de.MO) <www.de-mo.org>. /// PROGRAMMING: Arnaud Icard. /// TOOLS: Macromedia Flash, php, MySQL, film, natural sound
effects. /// COST: 120 hours. /// MAINTENANCE: 1 hour per month.

Concept

Los colores de la navegación representan la diversidad de los proyectos, que están ordenados por disciplinas. Cada cuadrado muestra un proyecto distinto. El minimalismo del diseño hace que el contenido destaque. //// I colori, durante la navigazione, rappresentano la varietà dei progetti accuratamente ordinati. Ogni quadrato mostra un progetto differente. Il design minimale serve per svelare il contenuto. //// As cores na navegação representam a diversidade de projectos, organizados tematicamente. Cada um dos quadrados constitui um projecto diferente. O design minimalista faz sobressair o conteúdo.

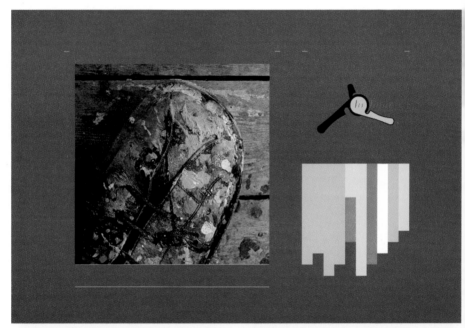

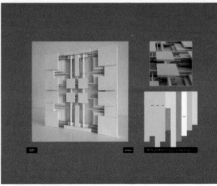

Infos

DESIGN AND PROGRAMMING: Jurgen Vanbrabant [Hipatrip]. /// **AWARDS:** Wow-Factor SOTW, Topten flash-es.net. /// **TOOLS:** Macromedia Flash, Action-script. /// **COST:** a lot of freetime. /// **MAINTENANCE:** 4 hours per month.

GERMANY

2004

HUIDI LAUHOFF

www.huidi-lauhoff.de

Minimalista y centrada en lo esencial: así es la presentación que Scholz & Volkmer hace en Internet de la nueva colección otoño-invierno de Huidi Lauhoff. //// Ridotta all'essenziale – così Scholz & Volkmer presentano in rete la nuova collezione autunno/inverno dello stilista di Wiesbaden, Huidi Lauhoff. //// Conciso e centrado no essencial – é desta forma que a Scholz & Volkmer apresenta na Internet a nova colecção feminina para o Outono/Inverno da estilista Huidi Lauhoff.

DESIGN: Scholz & Volkmer. /// PROGRAMMING: Flash Programming: Oliver Hinrichs; Technical Direction: Thorsten Kraus. /// AWARDS: Annual Multimedia Award, Communication networked Award of the German Designer Club (Silver). /// TOOLS: html, Macromedia Flash, xml. /// COST: 45 days.

73 · BEST PORTFOLIOS

HUT SACHS STUDIO

www.hutsachs.com

Concept

Porfolio de fotografías de proyectos. Navegación arquitectónica e intuitiva. //// Un sito portfolio fotografico, dotato di una navigazione architettonica ed intuitiva. //// Site dedicado a um portfólio fotográfico com uma navegação arquitectónica e intuitiva.

Infos

DESIGN AND PROGRAMMING: Knowawall Design <www.knowawall.com>. /// TOOLS: Macromedia Flash, html. /// COST: 90 hours. ///
MAINTENANCE: 5 hours per month.

HW PHOTOGRAPHY

www.hwphotography.com

Concept

Sencillo para un principiante, flexible para un experto. //// *Semplice per un principiante, flessibile per un esperto.* //// **Simples para um principiante, flexível para um especialista.**

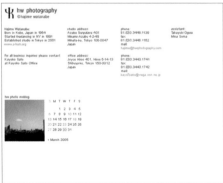

Infos

DESIGN AND PROGRAMMING: Hitoshi Okazaki (FIRM NOT NAMED YET) <www.firmnotnamedyet.com>. /// AWARDS: I.D. Magazine Interactive Media Design Review (Honorable Mention). /// TOOLS: Macromedia Flash, Movable Type. /// COST: 200 hours. /// MAINTENANCE: 1 hour per month.

HYBRIDWORKS

www.hybridworks.jp

Concept

Esta web, sin un concepto unificado, contiene gráficos, ilustraciones, animaciones, etc., repletos de humor. //// *Senza un concept unitario, il sito contiene grafica, illustrazioni, animazioni, e altre cose piene d'umorismo.* //// **Sem qualquer conceito unificador, este site contém gráficos, ilustrações, animações, etc., plenos de humor.**

Infos

DESIGN AND PROGRAMMING: Masaki Hoshino (HYBRIDWORKS). /// **TOOLS:** Adobe Photoshop, Adobe Illustrator, Macromedia Flash, xml. /// **COST:** 2 years. /// **MAINTENANCE:** 1-2 weeks per year.

IDIOM 3 MEDIA

www.idiom3.com

Concept

La idea de partida era crear un ambiente agradable para exponer los trabajos realizados y que fuera a la vez funcional y estético. //// L'idea fondamentale era creare un'atmosfera piacevole che mettesse in mostra il lavoro ma conservando anche funzionalità e senso estetico. //// A ideia subjacente a este site foi a de criar um ambiente agradável em que, para além de se expor o trabalho, se mantém simultaneamente a total funcionalidade e a estética.

Infos

DESIGN AND PROGRAMMING: John Cruz (Idiom 3 Media). /// AWARDS: Plasticpilots. /// TOOLS: Macromedia Flash, html. /// COST: 20 hours. /// MAINTENANCE: 5 hours per month.

ILLUSTRATOR.BE

www.illustrator.be

Concept

Esta web es una metáfora de las mesas de luz sobre las que los ilustradores solían trabajar en los viejos tiempos. //// La metafora del sito è simboleggiata da una "light box" che gli illustratori usavano in passato per realizzare i loro lavori. //// A metáfora do site é uma "caixa física leve" em que os ilustradores antigamente se sentavam para trabalhar.

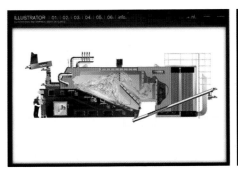 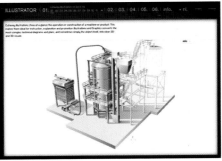

Infos

DESIGN AND PROGRAMMING: group94 <www.group94.com>. /// TOOLS: Macromedia Flash. /// COST: 3 weeks. /// MAINTENANCE: 1 day every 6 months.

INBREDBOY

www.inbredboy.com

Concept

Un día, un joven deforme de ojos saltones se pierde en una ciénaga. Descubre que tiene talento artístico y decide hacerse un pequeño porfolio con los retales y cachivaches que va encontrando por ahí. //// C'era una volta un ragazzo deforme e con gli occhi di fuori che si era perso in una palude. Scoprì un talento artistico e si realizzò un portfolio con le cianfrusaglie che trova in giro. //// Um rapaz deformado e com olhos esbugalhados perde-se nos pântanos. Descobre que tem talento para a arte e concebe um pequeno portfólio a partir dos restos que encontra no chão.

Infos

DESIGN: Cameron Wilson (Inbredboy). /// PROGRAMMING: Christian Ayotte. /// AWARDS: Digital Marketing Awards (Gold), Cannes Cyber Lion (Short List). ///
TOOLS: html, Macromedia Flash, dhtml, xml. /// CONTENT: music, film, etc. /// COST: 300 hours.

J6 STUDIOS

www.j6studios.com

Concept

J6Studios.com se creó como el lugar donde puedo almacenar mis ideas e intereses y mostrárselos al resto del mundo. //// J6Studios.com è stato creato per archiviare e mostrare le mie idee e i miei interessi al resto del mondo. //// O J6Studios.com foi criado como um local onde posso armazenar as minhas ideias e interesses e mostrá-los ao resto do mundo.

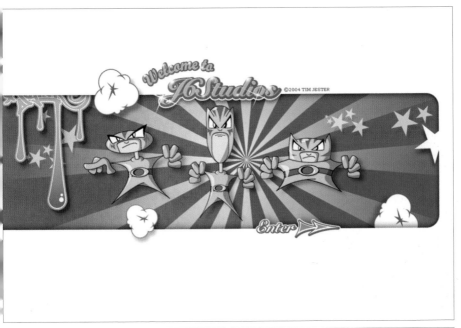

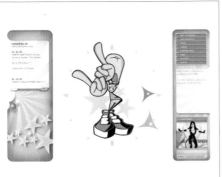

Infos

DESIGN: Tim Jester (J6Studios). /// PROGRAMMING: Tim Jester and Neal Desai. /// TOOLS: html, Macromedia Flash, music, xml. /// COST: the cost was zero. It was all done in my spare time. /// MAINTENANCE: it takes about 3 minutes for a new image, icon and text to be uploaded to the site.

JAN KNOFF PHOTOGRAPHY

GERMANY

www.janknoff.de

2004

Concept

El diseño no pretende mostrar su potencial mediante una navegación complicada, así que la página está elaborada con Flash y las imágenes se actualizan de forma automática. //// Il design non intende fare sfoggio di potenza con una navigazione complicata, perciò la pagina è costruita con Flash in modo che le immagini siano aggiornate automaticamente. //// O design baseia-se na intenção de não prejudicar o efeito das fotografias através de uma navegação complicada. Deste modo, este site em Flash assegura que, em caso de actualização, a navegação se adapte automaticamente.

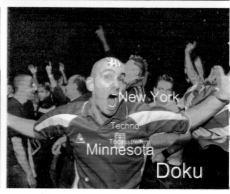

Infos

DESIGN: Jan Knoff and Wolfgang Kohlert. /// **PROGRAMMING:** Wolfgang Kohlert <www.cybercartoon.de>. ///
TOOLS: html, Macromedia Flash. /// **COST:** 136 hours.

JASON SIU & CO

www.jasonsiu.com

Concept

Di lo que piensas. //// Di quello che ti passa per la mente. //// **Diz o que pensas.**

Infos

DESIGN: DHKY <www.dhky.com> and Jason Siu. /// **PROGRAMMING:** DHKY. /// **AWARDS:** FWA. /// **TOOLS:** Adobe Photoshop, Adobe Illustrator, Macromedia Flash. /// **COST:** 2 months. /// **MAINTENANCE:** 2-3 hours every 2 month.

JEEDOUBLEU DESIGN

CANADA
2004

www.jeedub.com

Concept

En esta web quería visualizar el esfuerzo de los diseñadores por ser originales y «romper esquemas». //// Il concept del sito è visualizzare la lotta che i designer affrontano, cercando di pensare "outside the box". //// Na base deste site, está a ideia de visualizar a luta que os designers travam, tentando pensar "No Exterior Da Caixa".

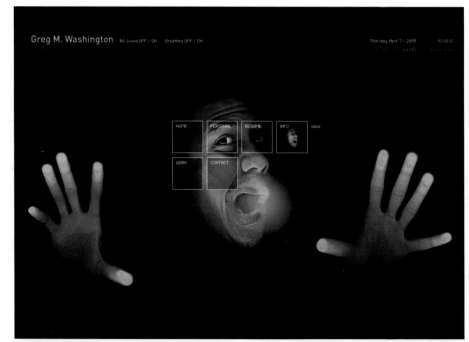

Infos

DESIGN AND PROGRAMMING: Greg M. Washington (JEEDUB). /// **AWARDS:** FWA, TINY, Flash Forward Festival. /// **TOOLS:** Adobe Illustrator, Adobe Photoshop, Adobe Premier, Macromedia Dreamweaver, Macromedia Flash, Actionscript, php, html, Javascript, music. /// **COST:** 20 hours. /// **MAINTENANCE:** 4 hours per month.

JENS GOERLICH PHOTO

www.jens-goerlich.de

El minimalismo de la navegación y de los elementos informativos debería servir para centrar toda la atención en el principal contenido de la web: las fotografías de Jens. //// La riduzione della navigazione e degli elementi informativi dovrebbe condurre ad una maggiore enfasi sul contenuto principale del sito, la fotografia di Jens. //// De forma a permitir uma maior concentração no conteúdo principal do site - a fotografia de Jens - optou-se por reduzir o espaço de navegação e os elementos informativos.

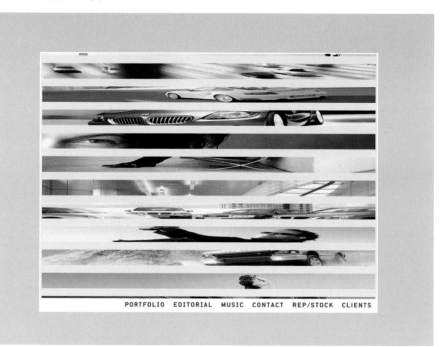

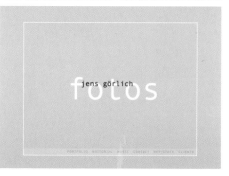

DESIGN AND PROGRAMMING: Amin Weber <www.amination.net>. /// TOOLS: Macromedia Flash, html, scanned images of slide- and negative film. /// COST: 50 hours. /// MAINTENANCE: 5 hours per month.

Concept

Al utilizar las fotografías como inspiración para una ilustración y después presentar la fotografía y la ilustración como una única experiencia interactiva, logramos una efecto emocionante e inolvidable. //// Abbiamo realizzato un'esperienza avvincente e indimenticabile, usando le foto come fonte d'ispirazione per un'illustrazione e presentando poi il tutto come un unico evento interattivo. //// Ao usar as fotografias como inspiração para uma ilustração e apresentar de seguida as fotografias e a ilustração como uma experiência interactiva, conseguimos criar uma experiência muito envolvente e memorável.

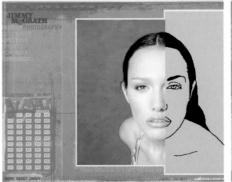

Infos

DESIGN: Todd Purgason, Luis Escoril, Paul Drohan, Mike Hanson, Nate Smith and Shant Parseghian (Juxt Interactive) <www.juxtinteractive.com>. /// **PROGRAMMING:** Todd Purgason. /// **AWARDS:** One show, Cannes Cyber Lion. /// **TOOLS:** Macromedia Flash. /// **COST:** too many to count.

JOE VAUX, MY HAPPY PLACE

USA
2003

www.joevaux.com

Concept

Quería que la web tuviera características de mis cuadros además de vida propia. Los sonidos y la animación crean una atmósfera que creo que realza la presentación de mi trabajo. //// Volevo che il mio sito avesse le stesse qualità dei miei dipinti ma anche una vita propria. I suoni e le animazioni infondono un'atmosfera che per me esalta la presentazione delle opere. //// Quis que o site tivesse algumas das características das minhas pinturas e vida própria. Os sons e a animação criam um ambiente que, no meu entender, realça a apresentação do meu trabalho.

Intos

DESIGN: Squidhaven L.L.C. <www.squidhaven.com>. /// PROGRAMMING: Tom Martin. /// TOOLS: html, Macromedia Flash. /// COST: 100 hours. ///
MAINTENANCE: $50 per month.

JOHN PARKER PHOTOGRAPHY

www.johnparker.biz

Concept

Una navegación sencilla pero eficaz para exponer las imágenes. //// *Navigazione semplice ed efficace per la presentazione d'immagini.* //// Navegação simples mas eficaz para a apresentação de imagens.

Infos

DESIGN: Chris Christodoulou (Saddington & Baynes) <www.sb-showcase.com>. /// PROGRAMMING: Duncan Hart. /// TOOLS: html, Macromedia Flash.

JULIAN WATSON AGENCY

www.julianwatsonagency.com

Concept

Un entorno fluido y relajado para contemplar la obra de los artistas. //// *Un ambiente fluido e sereno per osservare le opere degli artisti.* //// Um ambiente fluido e calmante para apreciar o trabalho dos artistas.

Infos

DESIGN: underwaterpistol <www.underwaterpistol.com>. /// PROGRAMMING: Gary Carruthers and Gary Belton. /// TOOLS: html, Macromedia Flash, php, MySQL. /// COST: 200 hours. /// MAINTENANCE: 4 hours per month.

Concept

El objetivo era lograr un sistema de navegación muy discreto, en el que no hubiera nada que distrajera la atención de las fotografías. ////
Lo scopo era rimuovere tutti gli ostacoli attraverso una navigazione discreta e far parlare la fotografia. //// O nosso objectivo consistiu em deixar que a navegação discreta removesse todos os elementos confusos e fizesse com que a fotografia surgisse em primeiro plano.

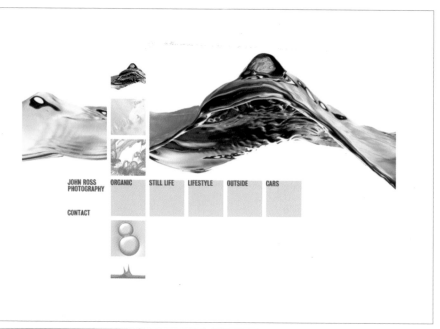

Infos

DESIGN: Toby Stokes and Dominic McMahon (Pretty) <www.prettystudio.co.uk>. /// PROGRAMMING: Simon Dixon. /// TOOLS: Macromedia Flash. ///
COST: 80 hours. /// MAINTENANCE: 6 hours every 6 months

JULIE WEST ILLUSTRATION

www.juliewest.com

Concept

La web se creó para que fuera austera y sencilla, pero sin dejar de reflejar el estilo gráfico de la artista en todo momento. //// Creato per essere semplice e chiaro, tutto il sito riflette però lo stile illustrativo dell'artista. //// Concebido para ser organizado e simples, não deixa de reflectir o estilo de ilustração do artista ao longo do site.

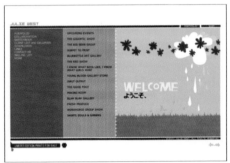 

Infos

DESIGN: Julie West. /// TOOLS: php, MySQL, html, CSS. /// COST: 40 hours. /// MAINTENANCE: 2 hours per week.

KARINA BEDNORZ PHOTO

www.karinabednorz.de

Concept

Un exterior preciso y austero que facilita la visión de conjunto de los porfolios. //// Un involucro preciso e senza sbavature, che permette una facile visione d'insieme dei portfolio presentati. //// Uma estrutura clara e precisa que permite uma fácil visão geral dos portfólios apresentados.

Infos

DESIGN AND PROGRAMMING: Rune Høgsberg <www.adoptdesign.com>. /// AWARDS: FWA, TAXI. /// TOOLS: Macromedia Flash. /// COST: 2.200 € /// MAINTENANCE: 1 hour per month.

Concept

Sencilla y elegante para asegurarse de que el diseño no reste fuerza a las imágenes. //// *Semplice* ed elegante, assicura che il design non disturbi la forza delle immagini. //// Simples e elegante, garantindo que o design não põe em causa a força das imagens.

Infos

DESIGN: underwaterpistol <www.underwaterpistol.com>. /// **PROGRAMMING:** Gary Carruthers and Gary Belton. /// **TOOLS:** html, Macromedia Flash, php, MySQL. /// **COST:** 240 hours. /// **MAINTENANCE:** 6 hours per month.

KDLAB

www.kdlab.net

Concept

Una estructura definida por densidades de transparencia que permiten observar el contenido en una distribución esmerada pero discreta. ////
Una struttura, definita attraverso vari gradi di trasparenza, permette la visione dei contenuti in modo dettagliato e consente di non distrarsi dal contenuto a fuoco. //// Uma estrutura que se define pela densidade da transparência permitindo que se veja o conteúdo num arranjo pormenorizado, caracterizando-se, no entanto, pelo facto de não distrair do conteúdo principal.

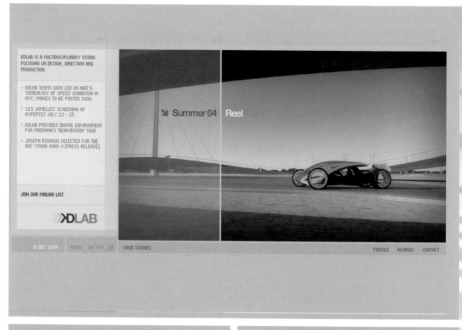

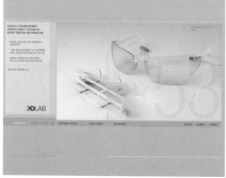

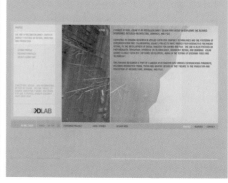

Infos

DESIGN AND PROGRAMMING: Dean DiSimone (KDLAB). /// AWARDS: Web Expo Siggraph. /// TOOLS: html, Macromedia Flash, mp3, Quicktime.

Concept

Concebida para sumergir al visitante en el reino mandinga, despertando sus sentidos con música e imágenes interactivas de África. //// È concepito per immergere l'utente nel regno di Manding stimolando i suoi sensi con musica e immagini africane interattive. //// Concebido para estimular os sentidos do utilizador com música e imagens interactivas africanas, enquanto visita o reino de Manding.

Infos

DESIGN: dunun <www.dunun.com>. /// PROGRAMMING: Micael Reynaud. /// AWARDS: fcukstar.com, TINY. /// TOOLS: Macromedia Flash, php, html. /// CONTENT: interactive music, photo, text, video. /// COST: 110 hours. /// MAINTENANCE: 5 hours per month.

KIRSTEN ULVE ILLUSTRATION USA

www.kirstenulve.com 2000

Concept

Alegre y vital. Para el porfolio quería colores primarios intensos y luminosos (mis dibujos) sobre un fondo negro. Y, además, ianimaciones y música! //// Chiaro e intenso. Ho scelto un effetto "Lite Brite" in cui il colore saturato in RGB (i miei disegni) risaltasse su uno sfondo nero nelle sezioni del portfolio. In più, ho inserito musica e animazioni piacevoli! //// Clara e vívida. Na secção dos portfólios, quis criar uma sensação "Lite Brite" (brinquedo) com cores saturadas (os meus desenhos) sob um fundo inteiramente preto. Além disso, ainda há animação e música!

Infos

DESIGN: Kirsten Ulve. /// **PROGRAMMING:** site and movement by Mike Faivre <www.sweatboxdesign.com>. Sound by Chad Pearson. ///
TOOLS: Adobe Photoshop, Adobe Illustrator, Macromedia Dreamweaver, Macromedia Flash, Quicktime, xhtml, CSS, Pro Tools, Reason, Garage Band. ///
COST: 50-60 hours. /// **MAINTENANCE:** 1-2 hours per month.

NORBERT KNIAT PHOTO

www.kniat.de

Concept

Crear un sitio web rápido, bonito y fácil de utilizar, y que funciona sin una molesta interfaz... //// Un sito creato per essere veloce, bello e facile da usare e per funzionare senza un'interfaccia "tecnologica"... //// Criar um site rápido, bonito e fácil de usar e que trabalha sem um interface muito "técnico"...

Infos

DESIGN: Matthias Netzberger (Lessrain) <www.lessrain.com>. /// **PROGRAMMING:** Matthias Netzberger (Frontend) & Peter Pokorny (Backend). ///
TOOLS: Adobe Photoshop, Macromedia Flash, Macromedia Dreamweaver, xml. /// **CONTENT:** music, photos. /// **COST:** 50 hours. ///
MAINTENANCE: 10 hours per month.

KOLLEKTIEF INTERIOR

www.kollektief.be

Concept

El porfolio se presenta estructurado en paneles flotantes. El sistema de navegación consiste ni más ni menos que en un único botón que contiene todas las funciones. //// Presenta il portfolio attraverso un sistema di pannelli mobili. Il sistema di navigazione consiste in un solo bottone che contiene tutte le funzioni. //// O portfólio é apresentado num sistema de painéis flutuantes. A navegação realiza-se através de um botão único com todas as funções incorporadas.

Infos

DESIGN AND PROGRAMMING: group94 <wwwgroup94.com>. /// **AWARDS:** FWA (Site of the Day), TAXI (Site of the Day), Visueller Orgasmus (Top20 Sites). ///
TOOLS: Macromedia Flash, php. /// **COST:** 3 weeks. /// **MAINTENANCE:** 1 day every year.

KREATIVKOLLEKTIV

www.kreativkollektiv.de

Concept

El concepto básico consiste en contar con una estructura dinámica y modular que permita añadir nuevos contenidos y diseños en cualquier momento. //// Il concept principale è costituito da una costruzione dinamica e modulare in grado di consentire l'inserimento di contenuti e progetti in qualsiasi momento. //// A ideia base consiste numa construção dinâmica e modular que permite inserir novos conteúdos e designs, a qualquer momento.

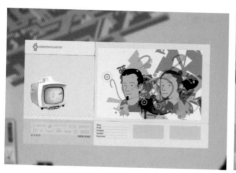 

Infos

DESIGN: Stefan Richter and André Grünhoff [Kreativkollektiv]. /// PROGRAMMING: Karsten Koch [Kreativkollektiv]. /// TOOLS: Macromedia Flash. /// CONTENT: audio, video, text. /// COST: 200 hours. /// MAINTENANCE: 10 hours per month.

LA FILLE D'O

www.lafilledo.com

Concept

Es sexy. Calentita. Un poco mala. No tengas miedo... Pincha y «entra». //// È sensuale, affascinante, con un pizzico di trasgressione. Non abbiate paura a usare il mouse e cliccate! //// Simplesmente sexy. Lascivo. Uma pitada de maldade. Não tenha medo de usar o rato e fazer **click**!

Infos

DESIGN: Stijn Pauwels [Milkandcookies] <www.milkandcookies.be>. /// PROGRAMMING: Milkandcookies. /// TOOLS: Macromedia Flash, Adobe Photoshop, and dirty pictures! /// COST: 2 weeks. /// MAINTENANCE: a lot!

Concept

Me ponía a escuchar discos antiguos con las canciones de Marilyn Monroe y me imaginaba cómo debía de ser el ir conduciendo un Chevrolet rosa por la carretera. //// Ho sentito alcune vecchie incisioni con melodie cantate da Marilyn Monroe e mi ha fatto pensare a quali sensazioni poteva suscitare guidare una Chevrolet rosa sull'autostrada. //// Estava a ouvir velhos discos riscados de Marylin Monroe e pensava na sensação que devia ser conduzir naqueles dias um Chevrolet cor-de-rosa pela estrada fora.

Infos

DESIGN AND PROGRAMMING: 247 Media Studios <www.24-7media.de>. /// AWARDS: Flash Film Festival San Francisco. /// TOOLS: Macromedia Flash. /// COST: 40 hours. /// MAINTENANCE: none.

LENNY

www.lenny.com.br

Concept

El sitio consta de una página principal y otra adicional, en forma de ventana emergente, para cada nueva temporada del calendario brasileño de la moda. //// Un sito web principale e un hotsite extra per ogni nuova stagione del calendario della moda brasiliana. //// Um site principal com uma janela adicional dedicada a cada nova época do calendário da moda brasileira.

Infos

DESIGN: 6D estúdio <www.6destudio.com.br>. /// **PROGRAMMING:** Gabriel Marques [6D estúdio]. /// **TOOLS:** Macromedia Flash. /// **CONTENT:** films [fashion shows edited by 6D estúdio], music [ocean sounds edited by 6D estúdio]. /// **COST:** 240 hours. /// **MAINTENANCE:** 48 hours every 6 months.

LIFE BEACH

www.lifebeach.ee

Impresionante. Una web para recordar. Una navegación única. //// Uno straordinario sito da ricordare. Navigazione eccezionale. //// **Site impressionante e inesquecível. Navegação única.**

DESIGN: Sander Sellin (Lime Creative) <www.lime.ee>. /// **PROGRAMMING:** Sander Sellin and Vladimir Morozov /// **AWARDS:** styleboost.com. ///
TOOLS: Macromedia Flash, html. /// **COST:** 100 hours. /// **MAINTENANCE:** 5-15 hours per month.

LIME CREATIVE

www.lime.ee

Concept Un porfolio en forma de revista, austero y sencillo. Así las fotografías se muestran siempre en el orden adecuado. //// È un layout di rivista chiaro e semplice. L'idea della rivista è stata usata per archiviare nell'ordine corretto le illustrazioni fotografiche. //// Um layout claro e simples em forma de revista. Para arquivar correctamente as ilustrações fotográficas, recorreu-se à ideia da revista para a navegação.

Infos DESIGN: Vladimir Morozov, Sander Sellin (Lime Creative). /// PROGRAMMING: Sander Sellin. /// AWARDS: FWA (Site of the Day), fcukstars.com. /// TOOLS: Macromedia Flash, html. /// CONTENT: photos. /// COST: 70 hours. /// MAINTENANCE: 5-10 hours per month.

LITTLELOUD

www.littleloud.com

Queríamos algo basado en un paisaje y mostrar algunas de nuestras influencias cinematográficas. //// Abbiamo scelto una base ambientale in cui mostrare alcune delle nostre influenze cinematografiche. //// Quisemos conceber algo baseado no meio ambiente e mostrar também algumas das nossas influências cinematográficas.

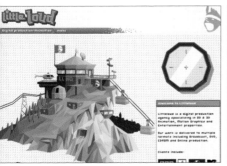 

DESIGN: David Jacklin, Darren Garrett, Iestyn Lloyd And Paul Simpson (LITTLELOUD). /// PROGRAMMING: Iestyn Lloyd. /// AWARDS: Best Creative Agency, Sussex Business Awards, Future Uk Internet Awards. /// TOOLS: Macromedia Flash, html, Quicktime, Adobe Photoshop, Adobe Illustrator, pens, pencils, and paper. /// COST: many hours and still working on it. /// MAINTENANCE: roughly 1 day or 2 each month.

MAGNET STUDIO

www.magnetstudio.com

La web se diseñó para que fuera lo más sencilla posible, pensando en que debían lucir los trabajos, no la web en sí. //// Il sito è progettato per la massima chiarezza, con l'idea di mettere in risalto il lavoro piuttosto che il sito stesso. //// O site foi concebido para ser o mais simples possível, pretendendo acima de tudo apresentar o trabalho em detrimento do próprio site.

DESIGN AND PROGRAMMING: Jon Black (Magnetstudio). /// TOOLS: Macromedia Flash. /// COST: 2 days. /// MAINTENANCE: 3 hours per month.

LOCOGRAFIX

www.locografix.com

Concept

El concepto y la navegación derivan del nombre Locografix, en el que «LOCO» es el acrónimo de Living Online Coorperation. //// La concezione e la navigazione derivano dal nome Locografix. (LOCO)grafix sta per 'Living Online Cooperation'. //// A concepção e a navegação derivam do nome Locografix. (LOCO)grafix significa "Living Online Coorperation".

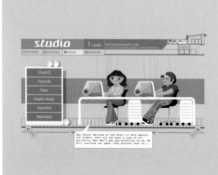

Infos

DESIGN: Locografix. /// PROGRAMMING: Jurgen van Zachten. /// AWARDS: Best Webpick Award, Daags (Site of the Month). /// TOOLS: html, Macromedia Flash, Adobe Illustrator. /// COST: 3 months. /// MAINTENANCE: 1 hour per month.

Concept

Trabajo en curso. //// Lavori in corso. //// Trabalho em progressão.

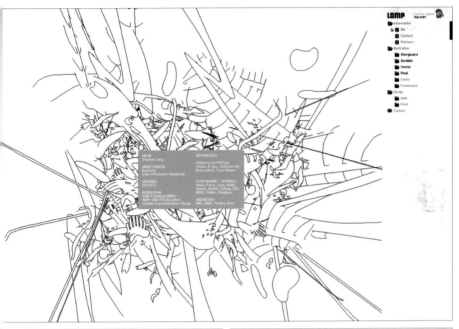

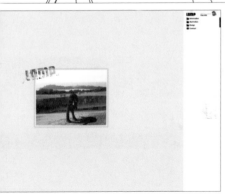

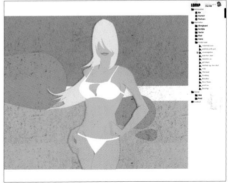

DESIGN AND PROGRAMMING: Stephan Lomp. /// AWARDS: FWA. /// TOOLS: Macromedia Flash, html. /// COST: I'm still working on it. ///
MAINTENANCE: 5-10 hours per month.

LOW PROFILE

www.lowprofile.ca

Concept

Facilitar el acceso a las obras y a los datos con simplicidad y elegancia y -lo más importante- ofrecer una experiencia creativa que potenciara la belleza de la obra de los artistas. //// Permettere un accesso facile al lavoro e alle informazioni in un modo semplice ed elegante e, la cosa più importante di tutte, offrire un'esperienza creativa capace di valorizzare le opere degli artisti. //// Permitir um acesso fácil aos trabalhos e à informação de uma forma simples e elegante e, o mais importante, oferecer uma experiência criativa que realçasse a qualidade do trabalho dos artistas.

Infos

DESIGN: Plank <www.plankdesign.com>. /// PROGRAMMING: Geoffrey Weeks. /// TOOLS: Macromedia Flash, Adobe Photoshop. /// COST: 100 hours. /// MAINTENANCE: average of 10 hours quarterly.

MAAG PICTURES

www.maagpictures.com

Concept

Una mirada divertida a las ilustraciones de Luke Magee. //// Uno sguardo allegro e piacevole tra le illustrazioni di Luke Magee. //// Uma visão extremamente divertida da ilustração de Luke Magee.

Infos

DESIGN AND PROGRAMMING: Luke Magee (Maag Pictures). /// AWARDS: Linkdup. /// TOOLS: Macromedia Flash, html. /// COST: 16 hours. /// MAINTENANCE: 2-3 hours per month.

MARTIN HOLTKAMP PHOTO

www.ma-ho.com

2001

Una caja de luz interactiva y una interfaz elástica que funciona con diapositivas dinámicas. El usuario puede ir pasando las diapositivas por la caja de luz con agilidad y considerable precisión. //// Una light box interattiva e un'interfaccia elastica che funziona grazie a sistemi dinamici di scorrimento. L'utente può far scivolare le immagini sulla light box in modo dinamico e abbastanza preciso. //// Uma caixa interactiva e um interface elástico que trabalha através de cursores dinâmicos. O utilizador pode deslocar imagens para a caixa de uma forma dinâmica e muito precisa.

DESIGN: Artificial Environments <www.ae-pro.com>. /// PROGRAMMING: Tom Elsner, Hilla Neske. /// AWARDS: we were given some awards, but I haven't kept records about it. /// TOOLS: html, Macromedia Flash.

MAX LAUTENSCHLÄGER

GERMANY

www.maxlautenschlaeger.de

2004

Una estructura simple pero elegante muestra los distintos trabajos, con una interfaz que el artista puede mantener y actualizar fácilmente. //// Un layout semplice, ma elegante, mostra la varietà dei lavori attraverso un'interfaccia che l'artista cura e aggiorna facilmente. //// Um layout simples mas elegante expõe a variedade de trabalhos, através de um interface que pode ser facilmente mantido e actualizado pelo artista.

DESIGN AND PROGRAMMING: Jan Illmann <www.jan-illmann.de>. /// TOOLS: Macromedia Flash, php, MySQL. /// COST: 35 hours.

MALCOLM TARLOFSKY

www.malcolmtarlofsky.com

Concept

Huir de la estructura clásica de la mayoría de los sitios web, con barras de menú a la izquierda o en los bordes superior o inferior, es un reto constante para cualquier diseñador. //// La navigazione principale dinamica è stata progettata per stare "out of the box". Allontanarsi dalla navigazione standard a sinistra, in alto, in basso è una sfida costante della progettazione. //// A navegação dinâmica principal foi criada para se situar "no exterior da caixa". Escapar à navegação padrão – à esquerda, em cima e em baixo – é um desafio constante para o design.

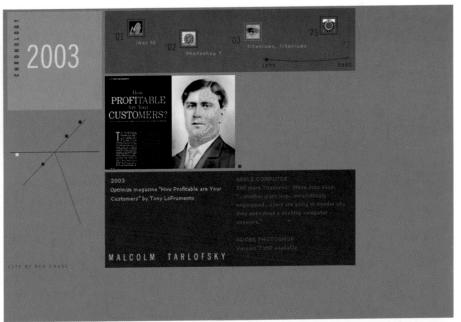

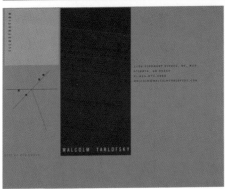
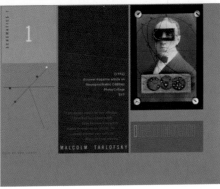

Infos

DESIGN: Deb Koch and Caroline Kavanagh (Red Canoe) <www.redcanoe.com>. /// PROGRAMMING: Deb Koch, Benjamin Kaubisch ///
AWARDS: HOW Interactive, Graphis Design Annual. /// TOOLS: Macromedia Flash, html, javascript.

MANIPULATOR STUDIOS

www.manipulator.com

Concept

Su estilo fotográfico requiere transiciones fluidas en la página del menú, en las páginas con imágenes y entre unas páginas y otras. Debido al tamaño de las imágenes, supuso todo un reto. //// Lo stile fotografico richiede delle transizioni fluide nella pagina di menù, nelle pagine delle immagini e tra una pagina e l'altra, per questo c'è stata una sfida dovuta alle dimensioni delle immagini. //// Para criar o estilo fotográfico foi necessário optar por transições fluidas na página do menu e nas páginas de imagens, bem como entre as diversas páginas. Um grande desafio tendo em consideração o tamanho das imagens.

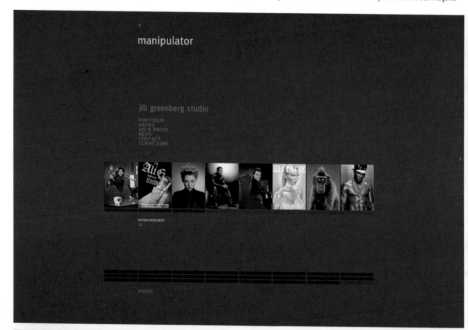

Infos

DESIGN AND PROGRAMMING: group94 <www.group94.com> /// AWARDS: FWA (Site of the Day), Wow-factor.com (Site of the Week). /// TOOLS: Macromedia Flash, php. /// COST: 5 weeks.

MARCO GROB PHOTO

www.marcogrob.com

Concept

Diseño reducido para dejar a las imágenes espacio suficiente para que hablen por sí mismas. Cada tira cuenta su propia historia. //// Un design ridotto che lascia abbastanza spazio alle figure per parlare da sole. Ogni striscia racconta la sua storia. //// Design reduzido que deixa suficiente espaço de expressão às imagens. Cada viagem conta a sua própria história.

Infos

DESIGN: KK,MG Advertising Agency <www.kk-mg.com>. /// PROGRAMMING: Patrick Schnyder. /// AWARDS: Moluv's Picks, k10k.net, etc. ///
TOOLS: html, Macromedia Flash, music, php. /// COST: 80 hours. /// MAINTENANCE: 2 hours per month.

Concept

Lo que más nos preocupaba, aparte de que las imágenes se cargaran rápido, era cómo presentar un sistema complejo de forma que se pudiera utilizar por intuición. //// Oltre ad immagini dal caricamento veloce, la preoccupazione principale del sito è presentare un sistema complesso in modo che sia il più intuitivo possibile da usare. //// Para além de imagens que se carregam rapidamente, a principal preocupação consistiu aqui em saber como apresentar um sistema complexo da forma mais intuitiva possível para o utilizador.

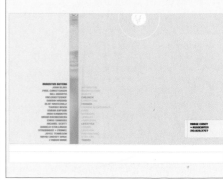

Infos

DESIGN: group94 (in collaboration with Liska NY) <www.group94.com>. /// **PROGRAMMING:** group94. /// **AWARDS:** FWA (Site of the Day), QBN (Certified on Newstoday), TAXI (Site of the Day), Wow-factor.com (Site of the Week). /// **TOOLS:** Macromedia Flash, php, MySQL. /// **COST:** 8 weeks.

MARIO LALICH PHOTOGRAPHY

www.mariolalich.com

Concept

La web de Mario Lalich es una auténtica interpretación de su estética. La sencilla navegación conduce al usuario sin esfuerzo hasta sus singulares fotografías, enmarcadas en colores vivos. //// Il sito di Mario Lalich è un'autentica interpretazione della sua estetica. La navigazione semplice introduce l'utente senza sforzo alle sue fotografie uniche, incorniciate da colori audaci. //// O site de Mario Lalich é uma verdadeira interpretação da sua estética. A navegação simples conduz facilmente os utilizadores às suas fotografias únicas, emolduradas em cores fortes.

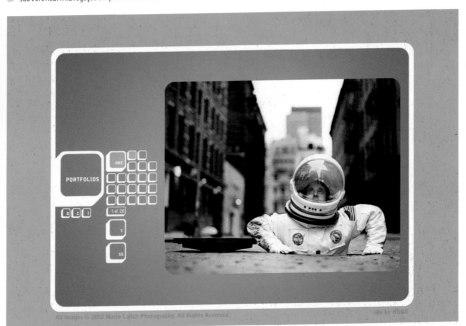

Infos

DESIGN AND PROGRAMMING: HUGE <www.hugeinc.com>. /// TOOLS: Macromedia Flash. /// COST: 2 months. /// MAINTENANCE: 5 hours every 2 months.

MARKESE PHOTOGRAPHY

www.markesephotography.com

Concept

Un diseño distintivo con un sistema de navegación fácil de abarcar y apoyado en una estructura de asombrosa longevidad. //// Un design distintivo con un sistema di navigazione facile da capire supportato da un layout di longevità sorprendente. //// Design distintivo com um sistema de navegação fácil de compreender com base num layout com uma longevidade incrível.

Infos

DESIGN: Branislav S. Cirkovic (Revolution Interactive) <www.revolutioninteractive.com>. /// **PROGRAMMING:** Scott Ysebert. /// **AWARDS:** FWA, TINY (Site of the Week), DOPE, Visueller Orgasmus (Site of the Week). /// **TOOLS:** Macromedia Flash, html, php, xml, MySQL, MP3 (with original music by Rich Markese), Discreet 3D Studio Max, Adobe Photoshop, Adobe AfterEffects. /// **COST:** 350 hours. /// **MAINTENANCE:** all work is handled through an admin panel. The database is so easy to use that its under a minute to get a new photo in.

Concept

Esta web minimalista expande o contrae los marcos para adaptarlos a la forma y el tamaño de cada imagen. Las imágenes se presentan como si fueran a publicarse en papel. //// Essenziale, il sito si espande e contrasta per presentare ogni immagine come se fosse pronta per andare in stampa, in armonia con la sua costruzione originale. //// Este site minimalista expande-se e revela contrastes para apresentar cada imagem em sintonia com esta construção única. As imagens estão formatadas como se estivessem prontas a imprimir.

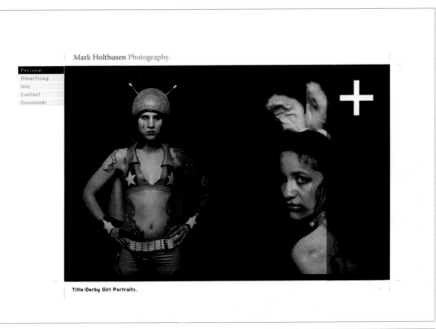

Title:Derby Girl Portraits.

Infos

DESIGN: Ever Growing Studio <www.evergrowing.net>. /// PROGRAMMING: Arron Bleasdale. /// TOOLS: Adobe Photoshop, Macromedia Flash, html, xml. /// COST: 80-100 hours.

Concept

Una sencilla exposición de los trabajos, fácil de seguir y que a la vez constituye una muestra de diseño funcional. //// *Un'esposizione del lavoro semplice e di facile navigazione che è anche un esempio di design funzionale.* //// **Uma apresentação simples dos trabalhos, que também são uma peça de design funcional. De fácil navegação.**

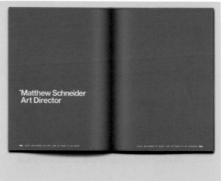

Infos

DESIGN: Matthew Schneider (Mattisimo). /// TOOLS: Adobe Photoshop, Macromedia Flash. /// COST: Many, many weekends and evenings. /// MAINTENANCE: many a night and weekend preparing files, cleaning up work and building. Truly a labor of love.

MICHEL HENAU

www.michelhenau.com

Concept

La idea básica consistía en presentar la colección de Michel Henau con austeridad y sencillez. La simplicidad y el minimalismo de la web concentran toda la atención del visitante en la colección. //// L'idea fondamentale era presentare la collezione di MH in modo semplice e chiaro: la configurazione e l'aspetto minimalista del sito permettono di captare completamente l'attenzione. //// A ideia subjacente consistiu na apresentação da colecção de MH de uma forma pura e simples, de maneira a que a elaboração e o ambiente minimalistas atraiam a atenção para a colecção.

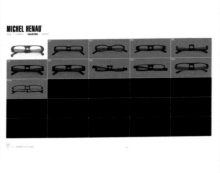

Infos

DESIGN: Deluxe Graphique <www.deluxe.be>. /// PROGRAMMING: Thomas Baert. /// AWARDS: TINY, Plasticpilots. /// TOOLS: Macromedia Flash, xml. /// COST: 120 hours. /// MAINTENANCE: that will depend on the growth of the collection the site is xml driven so it goes quite fast to update.

MIKE T ARTWORKS

USA
2002

www.miketartworks.com

Concept

Hip Hop Norman Rockwell. //// Hip Hop Norman Rockwell. //// Hip Hop Norman Rockwell.

Infos

DESIGN AND PROGRAMMING: Mike Thompson. /// TOOLS: Macromedia Flash. /// COST: too many.

114 · BEST PORTFOLIOS

MILES ALDRIDGE

www.milesaldridge.com

Concept

«Menos es más» es el concepto básico. Queríamos presentar las imágenes de Miles intactas, en todo su esplendor de colores básicos. //// "Meno è di più" è il concetto chiave. Abbiamo voluto presentare le immagini di Miles senza ritoccarle, in RGB e in tutto il loro splendore.. //// "Menos é mais" é o lema deste site. Quisemos apresentar as fotografias de Miles Aldridge sem quaisquer retoques, em toda a sua glória RGB (modelo de cores).

I am born in London in 1964

DESIGN AND PROGRAMMING: Hi-Res! <www.hi-res.net>. /// TOOLS: Macromedia Flash, Logic Pro, php, images, sound. /// COST: spread over almost 2 years, it's one of the longest running projects we have had so it's impossible to trace back how much time we spent.

MORTEN LAURSEN

www.mortenlaursen.com

Concept

Da la sensación de estar hojeando uno de esos fantásticos porfolios con tapas de piel de Morten Laursen. //// Riproduce la sensazione di curiosare qua e là tra i fantastici portfolio di pelle di Morten Laursen. //// **Reproduz a sensação de folhear os fantásticos portfólios de couro de Morten Laursen que nos são enviados.**

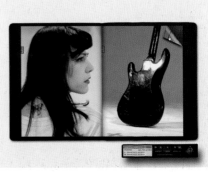

Infos

DESIGN AND PROGRAMMING: Weidemann Ltd. <www.weidemann.com>. /// **TOOLS:** Macromedia Flash, html, xml, CMS. /// **CONTENT:** sound, music, video. /// **MAINTENANCE:** maintained for free by owner using CMS.

Concept

Las fotografías tienen un importante papel en la estructura de esta web y unifican sus contenidos con los de la campaña publicitaria en la prensa. //// Le fotografie svolgono un ruolo molto importante nella costruzione di questo sito web, e uniscono il contenuto della web alla campagna pubblicitaria per la stampa. //// As fotografias desempenham um papel importante na construção deste site e ligam o conteúdo Web à campanha publicitária para a imprensa.

Design: Roberto Crippa <www.blover.com>. /// Programming: Dario Tubaldo. /// Tools: html, Macromedia Flash, Adobe Photoshop. /// Cost: 150 hours. //// Maintenance: 10 hours per month.

NEUMEISTER + PARTNER

www.neumeister-partner.de

Concept

Esta web elegante y de estructura sencilla transmite la filosofía del diseño de N+P: soluciones inteligentes, creativas y duraderas para proyectos de alta tecnología y alta calidad. //// Un sito strutturato in modo chiaro ed elegante trasmette la filovia di design di N+P: soluzioni intelligenti, creative e durevoli per progetti di alta qualità e tecnologia. //// O site elegante e claramente estruturado transmite a filosofia que a N+P aplica ao design: soluções inteligentes, criativas e duradouras para projectos de alta tecnologia e alta qualidade.

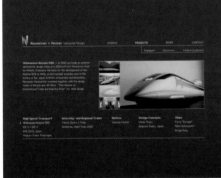

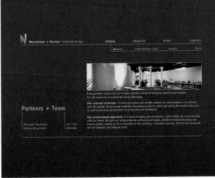

Infos

DESIGN: Joana Leal (Neumeister + Partner Industrial Design). /// **PROGRAMMING:** Christopher N. Friedmann (DESIGN : INSTINKT). /// **AWARDS:** Golden Web Award. /// **TOOLS:** Macromedia Flash, Adobe Photoshop, Allaire Homesite, Adobe Acrobat, html, JavaScript, VBS, Action Script. /// **COST:** 180 hours. /// **MAINTENANCE:** 30 hours every year.

NEW EZRA

Ofrece dos versiones a la vez: una interactiva, optimizada para Flash, y otra en HTML que cumple los estándares de la W3C y está centrada en la facilidad de uso. //// Il sito esplora una versione interattiva con Flash e, soddisfacendo gli standard, anche una versione in xhtml concentrata invece sull'utilizzabilità. //// Explora tanto o Flash interactivo como as formas de utilização centradas na versão xhtml, providenciando os padrões necessários.

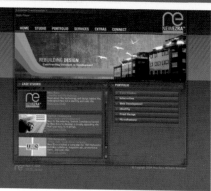

DESIGN AND PROGRAMMING: Jonathan Moore (New Ezra). /// AWARDS: Web Standards Award, Kirupa (Site of the Week), TINY /// TOOLS: xhtml, CSS, W3C Standards Compliance, php, Macromedia Flash, xml. /// COST: 60 hours. /// MAINTENANCE: 5 hours per month.

NINJACRUISE

www.ninjacruise.com

Concept NinjaCruise es un espacio en Internet en continua evolución. La navegación es un reflejo del estilo visual de cada actualización. //// NinjaCruise è uno spazio on-line in continua evoluzione. La navigazione riflette lo stile visivo d'ogni aggiornamento. //// A NinjaCruise é um espaço online em constante evolução. A navegação é uma reflexão do estilo visual de cada update.

Infos DESIGN AND PROGRAMMING: Matthew Curry (NinjaCruise). /// AWARDS: Coolstop.com, American Design Awards (Gold). /// TOOLS: Macromedia Flash, html. /// COST: thousands! /// MAINTENANCE: 5-30 hours a week.

Concept

Exposición de fotografías con una navegación divertida. //// Una presentazione fotografica con una navigazione divertente. //// Apresentação de fotografias com uma navegação divertida.

DESIGN AND PROGRAMMING: Are Bu Vindenes <www.arervindenes.com>. /// TOOLS: Macromedia Flash, html. /// COST: 40 hours. ///
MAINTENANCE: 1 hour per month.

Concept

Un porfolio en línea claro, sencillo y austero que produce la misma sensación que uno impreso. //// Un portfolio chiaro, semplice e senza difetti che sembra stampato. //// Portfólio claro, simples e puro que dá a sensação de estar impresso.

DESIGN: Chris Christodoulou (Saddington & Baynes) <www.sb-showcase.com>. /// **PROGRAMMING:** Duncan Hart. /// **TOOLS:** html, Macromedia Flash.

Infos

Todo se redujo a lo imprescindible; elementos como una sutil gama de grises, una animación suave y una navegación discreta e intuitiva logran que los visitantes se concentren en las fotos. //// Tutto è stato ridotto all'essenziale: degli elementi quali la tenue gamma di grigi, una morbida animazione e una navigazione discreta e intuitiva mantengono l'attenzione del visitatore centrata esclusivamente sulle sue fotografie. //// Tudo foi reduzido ao essencial; elementos como a subtil paleta cinzenta, a animação lustrosa e a navegação discreta e intuitiva fazem com que os utilizadores apenas se concentrem nas fotografias.

DESIGN AND PROGRAMMING: Lawrence Aaron Buchanan <www.lab-media.com>. /// AWARDS: Linkdup, TINY, Plasticpilots (Two Star), fcukstar.com, Ades Design, Strange Fruits, American Design Award, Net Inspiration, Best Flash Designs, e-Creative, Cool Home Pages, Design Firms, GOUW, DOPE, DesignLinks.org. /// TOOLS: Macromedia Flash, html. /// COST: 60 hours. /// MAINTENANCE: 1 hour per month.

SAMO VIDIC PHOTOGRAPHY

www.onlysamo.com

Concept

La web se centra en las excelentes fotografías de Samo Vidic y hace hincapié en su claridad y concisión mediante el uso de diseños minimalistas. //// Il sito focalizza l'attenzione sull'eccellente fotografia di Samo Vidic, mettendo in risalto la chiarezza e la stringatezza attraverso l'uso di linee essenziali di design. //// O site centra-se na excelente fotografia de Samo Vidic, dando ênfase à sua claridade e concisão através do recurso a padrões de design minimalistas.

Infos

DESIGN: Webshocker <www.webshocker.net>. /// PROGRAMMING: Matjaz Valentar /// AWARDS: FWA, ITA, fcukstar.com, DOPE, King For a Week, and more. /// TOOLS: Macromedia Flash, Adobe Photoshop. /// COST: 60 hours.

Un entorno que representa mi forma de ver el mundo que me rodea y su influencia en mi trabajo. //// *Un ambiente che raffigura come io vedo il mondo che mi circonda e la sua influenza sul mio lavoro.* //// Um ambiente que representa a forma como encaro o mundo circundante e como este influencia o meu trabalho.

DESIGN: Pablo Marques. /// PROGRAMMING: Pablo Marques, Zé Rorshack and Flávio Ensiki. /// AWARDS: FWA, Bombshock, TINY. /// TOOLS: Adobe Photoshop, html, Macromedia Flash, xml, Sound Edition in Peak LE. /// COST: 200 hours. /// MAINTENANCE: 5-10 hours per month.

PETER FUNCH PHOTOGRAPHY

www.peterfunch.com

Concept

Un porfolio fotográfico de diseño austero que proyecta las fotografías con gran intensidad. //// Il portfolio di un fotografo dal design solido e ordinato che realizza formidabili fotografie. //// Portfólio de um fotógrafo num design severo e preciso que projecta as fotografias de uma forma poderosa.

Infos

DESIGN: Adoptdesign <www.apoptdesign.com>. /// AWARDS: Masterclass Student. /// TOOLS: Adobe Photoshop, html, Macromedia Flash. /// COST: 3 weeks. /// MAINTENANCE: zero till next update.

Concept

Menos es más. //// Meno è meglio. //// Menos é mais.

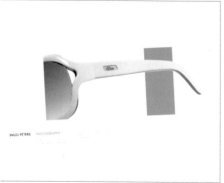

Infos

DESIGN: ZUM KUCKUCK <www.zumkuckuck.com>. /// PROGRAMMING: Werner Goldbach, Steven Schmidt and Daniel Rothaug. /// AWARDS: fcukstar.com, mypixeloryours.com, puraraza.net. /// TOOLS: Macromedia Flash, JavaScript, html. /// COST: 102 hours. /// MAINTENANCE: 3h every 3 months.

PHOTOPIX PHOTOGRAPHY

www.photopix.net

Concept

Esta página forma parte de una web fotográfica doble. Las dos páginas contienen un porfolio totalmente actualizable, funcionan con el mismo motor y tienen las mismas funciones. //// Questo sito fa parte di una web portfolio di due fotografi. Entrambi i siti presentano un portfolio completamente aggiornabile, basato sullo stesso dispositivo e con una funzionalità simile. //// Este site faz parte de um duplo site de apresentação dos portfólios de um fotógrafo. Ambos os sites dispõe de um portfólio totalmente actualizável, baseado no mesmo motor de site e com uma funcionalidade semelhante.

Infos

DESIGN AND PROGRAMMING: group94 <www.group94.com>. /// TOOLS: Macromedia Flash, php. /// COST: 5 weeks.

PIXELRANGER

www.pixelranger.com

Creé una experiencia basada en la manipulación de sonido e imagen, de modo que cualquiera pueda vivirla como si realmente estuviera ahí dentro.

//// Ho dato vita ad un'esperienza basata sulla manipolazione del suono e dell'immagine che ognuno potrebbe sperimentare come se si trovasse realmente lì.

//// Criei uma experiência baseada na manipulação de sons e imagem que qualquer um pode sentir como se a estivesse realmente a viver.

DESIGN AND PROGRAMMING: Shane Seminole Mielke <www.pixelranger.com>. /// AWARDS: FWA (Site of the Day). /// TOOLS: html, Macromedia Flash, xml, audio, photography. /// COST: 40 hours to design and create the core site. /// MAINTENANCE: 1 hour per month to update the portfolio.

Concept

La web se diseñó para que fuera muy «mínima». Pensé que no se trataba tanto de incluir montones de «extras» como de tener ideas interesantes que se pudieran expresar con simplicidad. //// Il sito è progettato per essere "minimalista": la questione non è usare una miriade d'elementi "extra" ma avere idee interessanti, che possono essere espresse in una forma semplice. //// O site foi concebido para ser muito "minimal". Considerei que o mais importante não é o recurso a um grande número de "extras", mas sim as ideias interessantes que podem ser expressas de uma forma simples.

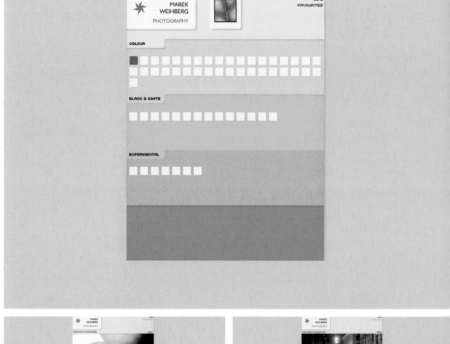

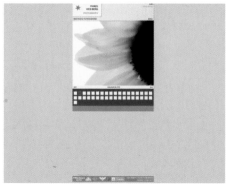

Infos

DESIGN AND PROGRAMMING: Marek Weihberg (Pixel Riot) <www.pixelriot.pl>. /// AWARDS: FWA (Site Of The Day), DOPE, e-Creative (Site Of The Day), NewWebPick, American Design Award. /// TOOLS: Macromedia Flash, xml. /// COST: 60 hours. /// MAINTENANCE: thanks to the use of xml keeping my site updated takes a little time. I only have to add a proper lines to the xml file and the site is automatically updated.

La idea básica de la web era que los usuarios aterrizaran en el planeta imaginario «planetB» para explorar los servicios de una productora especializada en anuncios televisivos. //// Il concept del sito era creare per gli utenti l'esperienza di un pianeta immaginario, "planetB", in cui sia possibile esplorare i servizi della casa di produzione specializzata in spot televisivi. //// Quisemos que os utilizadores pudessem sentir-se no planeta imaginário "planetB", em que podem explorar os serviços de uma empresa de produção especializada em anúncios televisivos.

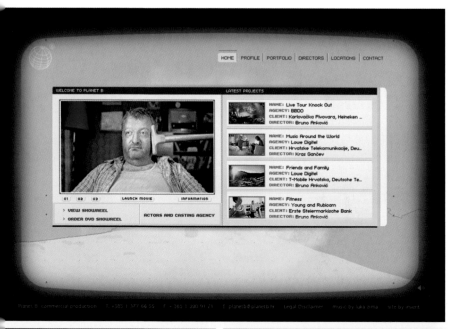

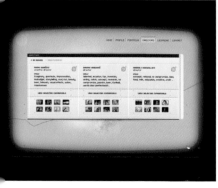

DESIGN: Igor Skunca (invent : multimedia studio) <www.invent.hr>. /// **PROGRAMMING:** invent : multimedia studio. /// **AWARDS:** Croatian Advertising Festival. /// **TOOLS:** Macromedia Flash, Macromedia Dreamweaver, Adobe Photoshop. /// **CONTENT:** music by Luka Zima; films by planetB. /// **COST:** 350 hours. /// **MAINTENANCE:** 25 hours per month.

PORTE-VOIX.COM

www.porte-voix.com

Concept

Un diseño muy claro y sencillo para que no eclipse las obras que contiene. //// Un design semplice e chiaro per non uccidere il lavoro mostrato al suo interno. //// Um design muito claro e simples para não oprimir o trabalho nele incluído.

Infos

DESIGN AND PROGRAMMING: Benoit Godde <www.porte-voix.com>. /// TOOLS: Macromedia Flash, html, dhtml, xml. /// COST: to much. /// MAINTENANCE: to much again—I love Sophie, my girlfriend.

PRECURSOR

www.precursorstudio.com

Concept

La web se diseñó para que fuera muy fácil de usar y para ensalzar las obras que muestra. Ni está sobrecargada ni abruma al visitante: contiene los trabajos y nada más. //// Il sito è stato progettato per essere molto facile da usare e per dare la massima importanza al lavoro che vi è contenuto. Non ha un design ingombrante o aggressivo, è in risalto il lavoro e nient'altro. //// O site foi concebido para ser fácil de utilizar e para dar a máxima importância ao trabalho nele incluído, não sendo o seu design nem excessivamente rebuscado nem básico: incide sobre os trabalhos e nada mais.

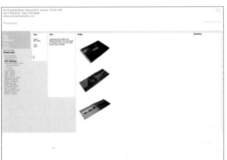 

Infos

DESIGN: Precursor. /// PROGRAMMING: Chris Bond and Jon Spain. /// TOOLS: Adobe Photoshop, Macromedia Fireworks, Macromedia Dreamweaver, dhtml, xml, asp. Content is an asp/xml based management system /// COST: 35 hours. /// MAINTENANCE: all updating is done in house and it varies from month to month

Su rostro angelical, cual gran ojo del paraíso, brilló intensamente y creó un claro de sol en aquel lugar sombrío. //// Il suo volto angelico splendeva lucente come il grande occhio del cielo e portò la luce tra le tenebre. //// A sua face de anjo brilhou intensamente como o grande olho do céu, e fez luzir um raio de sol num lugar sombrio.

DESIGN: Valentijn Destoop (Quidante). /// **PROGRAMMING:** Front-end: Thomas Spiessens; Back-end: Stefan Colins and Vic Rau. /// **AWARDS:** TAXI (Site of the Day), MultiMediaMadness (Best Web Application), Golden Website (Best Flash Designs), NewWebPick (Superpick of the World), DOPE, BD4D, fcukstar.com, LinkDup, De Lijst, Moluv's Picks. /// **TOOLS:** Macromedia Flash, xml, html. /// **COST:** 1 month. /// **MAINTENANCE:** 10 hours per month.

Concept

Esta web nació cuando realicé mi primer diseño gráfico. Es la recopilación de mis trece años de obra gráfica. //// Il sito è nato all'epoca del mio primo disegno. È la raccolta di tredici anni di lavoro come grafico. //// Este site foi criado quando completei o meu primeiro desenho gráfico e trata-se de uma compilação de 13 anos dedicados aos trabalhos gráficos.

Infos

DESIGN: Rafael de Barros Garcia. /// PROGRAMMING: Daniel Maia and Marcelo de Paula. /// TOOLS: html, Macromedia Flash. /// CONTENT: music, film. /// COST: over 1.000 hours. /// MAINTENANCE: 6 hours per month.

Concept

Esta página forma parte de una web fotográfica doble. Las dos páginas contienen un porfolio totalmente actualizable, funcionan con el mismo motor y tienen las mismas funciones. //// Il sito fa parte di una web portfolio di due fotografi. Entrambi i siti presentano un portfolio completamente aggiornabile, basato sullo stesso dispositivo e con una funzionalità simile. //// Este site faz parte de um site duplo de apresentação dos portfólios de um fotógrafo. Ambos os sites dispõe de um portfólio totalmente actualizável, baseado no mesmo motor de site e com uma funcionalidade semelhante.

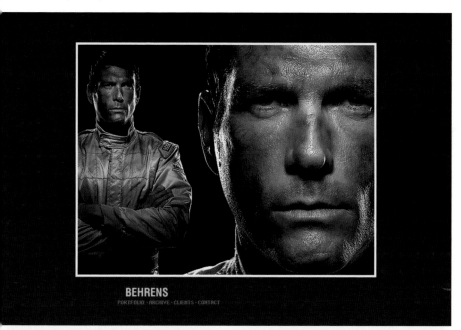

Script

DESIGN AND PROGRAMMING: group94 <www.group94.com>. /// AWARDS: axesart.com (Site of the day), wow-factor.com (Site of the week), e-Creative (Site of the day). /// TOOLS: Macromedia Flash, php. /// COST: 5 weeks.

RALF WENGENMAYR

www.ralfwengenmayr.com

Concept

El objetivo era dar a conocer las aptitudes como compositor de Ralf Wengenmayr y los proyectos que ha realizado hasta la fecha. //// L'obiettivo è stato quello di presentare i grandi meriti compositivi di Ralf Wengenmayr ed i progetti che ha finora realizzato. //// O objectivo consistiu em apresentar as vastas capacidades de Ralf Wengemayr como compositor e os projectos que realizou até ao momento.

Infos

DESIGN AND PROGRAMMING: SCHOLZ & VOLKMER <www.s-v.de>. /// AWARDS: Cannes Cyber Lion, Best of Business-to-Business, Red Dot Communication Design, EPICA, iF Interaction Design, HOW Interactive Design, Art Directors Club New York, International Web Page, One Show Interactive, ANDY, Clio, Design and Art Annual, London International Advertising Award. /// TOOLS: html, Macromedia Flash, xml. /// CONTENT: music, film.

Concept

Este sitio web se parece mucho a un porfolio fotográfico «físico». Para que la experiencia sea lo más auténtica posible, el menú sólo aparece cuando el usuario interactúa con el sitio. //// Il sito riproduce da vicino le sensazioni trasmesse da un portfolio fotografico reale. Per rendere l'esperienza più autentica possibile, la navigazione si rivela soltanto quando l'utente interagisce con il sito. //// O site dá a sensação de ser quase um portfólio físico do fotógrafo. De forma a manter a experiência o mais autêntica possível, a navegação apenas se revela quando o utilizador está a interagir com o site.

Intro

DESIGN AND PROGRAMMING: Matthias Netzberger (Lessrain) <www.lessrain.com>. /// AWARDS: Reboot, Golden Web, Platinum. /// TOOLS: Adobe Photoshop, Macromedia Flash, Macromedia Dreamweaver, xml, music, photos. /// COST: 100 hours. /// MAINTENANCE: 10 hours per month.

Concept

La navegación de 3 niveles, en forma de base de datos, es un sistema de cuadrados rojos en transformación. //// La navigazione a 3 livelli di profondità e database-driven è costituita da un sistema a ri expedient quadri rossi che si trasformano. Grazie all'intelligente sistema di preload, non c'è quasi mai bisogno di attendere all'interno del sito. //// A navegação com 3 níveis e estruturada numa base de dados consiste num sistema de quadrados vermelhos.

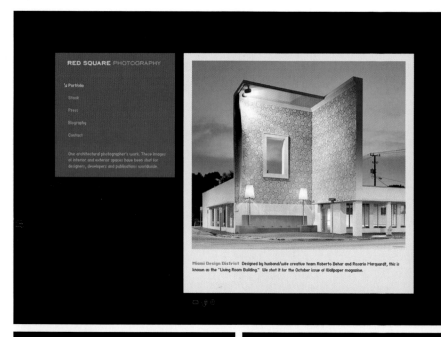

Infos

DESIGN AND PROGRAMMING: group94 <www.group94.com>. /// **TOOLS:** Macromedia Flash, php, MySQL. /// **COST:** 5 weeks.

Concept

Una escena típica de Hong Kong. //// Una scena campestre di Hong Kong. //// Uma cena local de Hong-Kong.

Layout

DESIGN: Tom Shum, Kevin Tsang, Andrew Lee <www.rice5.com>. /// **PROGRAMMING:** Daniel Yuen. /// **AWARDS:** HK 4As Interactive Awards - Best Use of Interactive Single (Silver), Bombshock, FWA (Site of the Day), American Design Award (Site of the Month) /// **TOOLS:** html, Macromedia Flash, xml. /// **COST:** 1 month. /// **MAINTENANCE:** 2-3 hours per month.

www.ronbergphoto.com

Concept

El propio texto serviría de menú de navegación para obtener toda la información pertinente, y la no tan pertinente, sobre Ron y su obra. //// Al posto delle tradizionali categorie (contatti, biografia, premi e così via), la copia stessa serve come strumento di navigazione per ottenere informazioni, pertinenti e non, su Ron e sul suo lavoro. //// O texto serviu como forma de navegação para aceder às informações pertinentes, ou nem tanto, sobre Ron Berg e o seu trabalho.

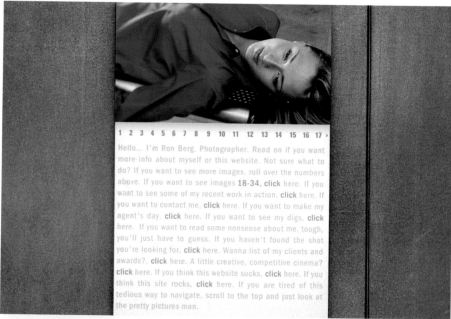

1 2 3 4 5 6 7 8 9 10 11 12 13 14 15 16 17 ›

Hello... I'm Ron Berg. Photographer. Read on if you want more info about myself or this website. Not sure what to do? If you want to see more images, roll over the numbers above. If you want to see images **18-34**, **click** here. If you want to see some of my recent work in action, **click** here. If you want to contact me, **click** here. If you want to make my agent's day, **click** here. If you want to see my digs, **click** here. If you want to read some nonsense about me, tough, you'll just have to guess. If you haven't found the shot you're looking for, **click** here. Wanna list of my clients and awards?, **click** here. A little creative, competitive cinema? **click** here. If you think this website sucks, **click** here. If you think this site rocks, **click** here. If you are tired of this tedious way to navigate, scroll to the top and just look at the pretty pictures man.

Infos

DESIGN: Todd Eaton (Mojo Studios) <www.mojostudios.com>; and Karen Knecht (KonnectDesign) <www.konnectdesign.com>. /// **PROGRAMMING:** Todd Eaton. /// **AWARDS:** FWA, fcukstar.com, DOPE, NewWebPick, TINY. /// **TOOLS:** Macromedia Flash, Macromedia Dreamweaver, Sorenson Squeeze, Adobe Premier, Adobe Audition, html, mp3, FLV. /// **COST:** 200 hours. /// **MAINTENANCE:** only minimal updating of images and videos.

ROYAL BOTANIA

www.royalbotania.com

Concept

El sistema es visual y permite navegar pinchando aquí y allá de las fotos de los productos a las especificaciones técnicas. //// Un sistema di click-through permette al visitatore di passare con facilità ed efficacia da immagini d'atmosfera alle schede tecniche dei prodotti e viceversa. Completano il sito un calendario d'eventi, uno store locator, un servizio di assistenza, eccetera. //// Um sistema visual para clickar permite ao visitante saltar fácil e eficientemente do imaginário atmosférico para as páginas com os produtos técnicos e vice-versa.

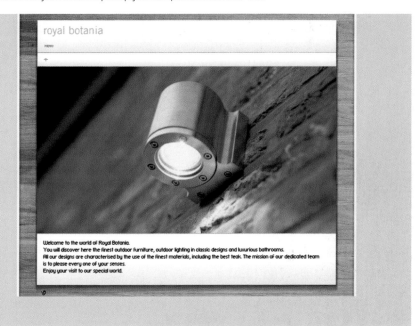

DESIGN AND PROGRAMMING: group94 <www.group94.com>. /// AWARDS: FWA (Site of the Day). /// TOOLS: Macromedia Flash, php, MySQL. /// COST: 7 weeks.

Concept

El máximo espacio para los fotógrafos y una tipografía enérgica, multicolor y alegre. //// Massimo spazio per la presentazione delle fotografie vs. stile tipografico audace, colorato e divertente. //// Espaço máximo para os fotógrafos apresentados, em conjugação com uma tipografia arrojada, colorida e alegre.

Infos

DESIGN AND PROGRAMMING: Tomas Celizna (dgu) www.dgu.cz. /// TOOLS: Macromedia Flash, amfphp, php, MySQL, html. /// COST: 90 hours. /// MAINTENANCE: 250 hours per month.

Concept

Presenta la obra de Sagmeister Inc. de forma clara y muy accesible. //// Il sito presenta il lavoro di Sagmeister Inc. in modo chiaro e facilmente accessibile. //// Apresenta os trabalhos de Sagmeister Inc. de uma forma clara e facilmente acessível.

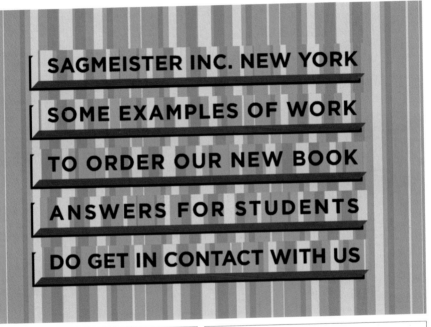

Infos

DESIGN: Sagmeister Inc. /// PROGRAMMING: Francisco J. Castro Lopez. /// TOOLS: Macromedia Flash. /// COST: 80 hours. /// MAINTENANCE: 1 hour per month.

SALVA CAMPILLO

www.salvacampillo.com

Concept

La idea era ser muy claros y dar el mayor protagonismo posible a las fotografías, con un sistema de navegación fácil e intuitivo. //// L'idea fondamentale è essere chiari e dare il massimo rilievo alle figure con un sistema di navigazione facile e intuitivo. //// Pretendeu-se aqui optar por uma grande clareza e dar o máximo relevo possível às fotografias, recorrendo a um sistema de navegação fácil e intuitivo.

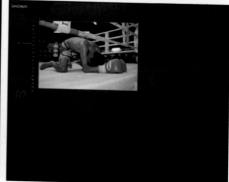

Infos

DESIGN AND PROGRAMMING: Diego Laredo de Mendoza <www.lary.it>. /// AWARDS: TINY, Plasticpilots (3 Stars), fcukstar.com, American Design Awards. /// TOOLS: Macromedia Flash, Macromedia Dreamweaver. /// COST: 100 hours. /// MAINTENANCE: 1-2 hours per month.

Concept

Una web completa donde exponer retoques creativos. //// Un sito completo per presentare ritocchi creativi. //// Um site polivalente para apresentar retoques criativos.

Infos

DESIGN AND PROGRAMMING: James Digby-Jones (Saddington & Baynes). /// AWARDS: IDEA Digital Imaging Interactive. /// TOOLS: html. /// MAINTENANCE: updated whenever new images are needed.

SCARYGIRL

www.scarygirl.com

Concept Una web divertida y dinámica donde se exhiben los juguetes Scarygirl y proyectos relacionados. //// Un sito rapido e divertente per esibire i giocattoli di Scarygirl ed i relativi progetti. //// Um site veloz e divertido para expor os brinquedos Scarygirl e projectos relacionados.

Infos **DESIGN:** Nathan J (Soap Creative) <www.nathanj.com.au>; <www.soap.com.au>. /// **PROGRAMMING:** Ashley Ringrose. /// **TOOLS:** html, Macromedia Flash. /// **COST:** 40 hours. /// **MAINTENANCE:** 5 hours per month.

Concept

Queríamos un diseño austero y sencillo que centrara la atención en el trabajo, sin por ello dejar de ofrecer al usuario una experiencia única y divertida. //// Abbiamo scelto un design chiaro e semplice, che focalizzasse l'attenzione sul lavoro svolto e che tuttavia rendesse l'esperienza dell'utente divertente e unica. //// Quisemos criar um design claro e simples centrado no nosso trabalho, mas de maneira a que os visitantes passem por uma experiência única e divertida.

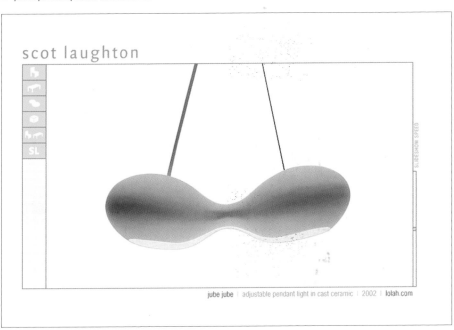

scot laughton

jube jube | adjustable pendant light in cast ceramic | 2002 | lolah.com

scot laughton

scot laughton

biography

Infos

DESIGN AND PROGRAMMING: Thomas Klepl (Pivot Design) <www.pivotdesign.ca>. /// TOOLS: Macromedia Flash. /// COST: 120 hours. /// MAINTENANCE: 2 hours per month.

THE ART OF SHAWN BARBER

www.sdbarber.com

Concept

Simplicidad gráfica; dejar que la obra hable por sí misma. //// *Semplicità grafica: il lavoro parla da solo.* //// **Simplicidade gráfica que deixa o trabalho falar por si.**

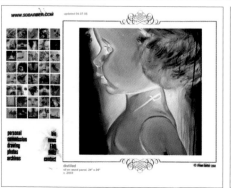

Infos

DESIGN AND PROGRAMMING: Shawn Barber. /// **TOOLS:** html, Adobe Golive.

Concept

El concepto arrancó de la campaña publicitaria de Sergio Rossi en la que se veía a las modelos reflejadas en espejos. La navegación es mínima y discreta, y complementa la estética de los diseños de Sergio Rossi. //// Il design concept aveva già avuto il via con la campagna pubblicitaria di Sergio Rossi, in cui l'immagine delle modelle si rifletteva su degli specchi. La navigazione è minimalista e non invasiva, e completa il design estetico di Sergio Rossi. //// A ideia teve origem na campanha publicitária de Sergio Rossi em que apresenta modelos reflectidos em espelhos. A navegação é minimalista e discreta, completando a estética de Sergio Rossi.

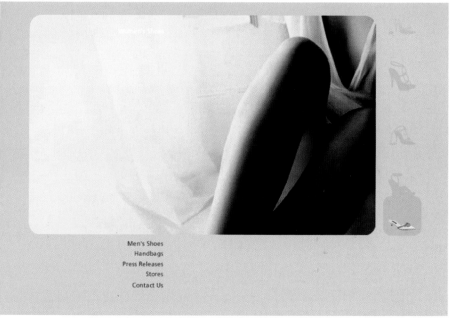

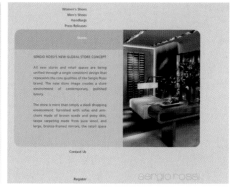

DESIGN: Vas Sloutchevsky (Firstborn) <www.firstbornmultimedia.com>. /// **PROGRAMMING:** Shea Gonyo and Josh Ott /// **TOOLS:** Macromedia Flash.

SHADOW AND LIGHT

USA
2004

Concept

Exposición interactiva de imágenes en blanco y negro que contiene una serie de 90 fotografías tomadas durante tres meses de viaje y estudios arquitectónicos por Europa y Escandinavia. //// Esposizione interattiva di fotografie in bianco e nero, che contiene una collezione di 90 fotografie scattate durante tre mesi di viaggi e studi d'architettura tra Europa e Scandinavia. //// Exposição de fotografia interactiva a preto e branco contendo uma coleoção de 90 fotografias tiradas durante três meses de viagem e estudos arquitectónicos através da Europa.

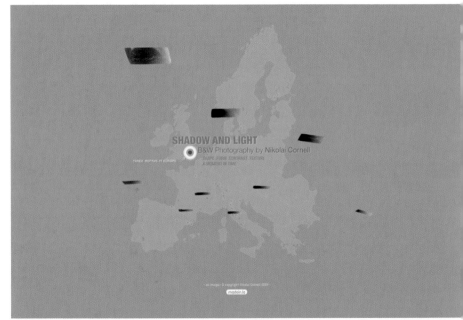

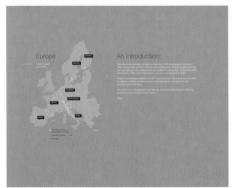

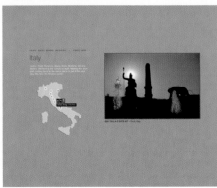

Infos

DESIGN AND PROGRAMMING: Nikolai Cornell (madeinLA) <www.madein.la>. /// AWARDS: I.D. Interactive Media Design Review (Bronze), STEP design 100, Flash in the Can Design and Technology Festival, Thailand New Media Art Festival, Yahoo Picks (Site of the Day), Flashkit. /// TOOLS: 35mm "analog" camera, Macromedia Flash, Adobe Photoshop, Adobe ImageReady. /// COST: I worked on the website on and off for 2 years. Really about 2 months of solid work. /// MAINTENANCE: maybe 1 hour a month answering emails.

Concept

La considero mi sitio de recreo personal y confío en que los visitantes se contagien de mi entusiasmo. //// *Lo concepisco come il mio parco giochi personale e spero che i visitatori percepiscano il mio entusiasmo.* //// Considero-o o meu pátio de recreio privado, e espero que os visitantes consigam partilhar o meu entusiasmo.

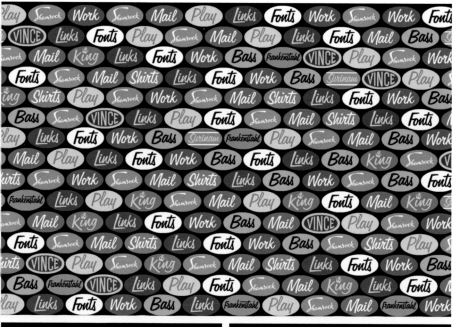

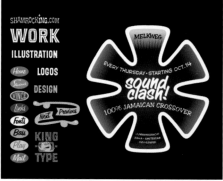

Infos

DESIGN: Jeroen Klaver (Shamrock Int.). /// TOOLS: Macromedia Flash. /// COST: 1 week. /// MAINTENANCE: That reminds me... should update again!

SHERRI O'CONNOR PHOTO

www.sherriphoto.com

Concept

Mediante la creación de una navegación intuitiva y el uso de la tecnología Flash, tratamos de convertirlo en toda una experiencia y de sumergir al usuario en las fotografías. //// Con una navigazione intuitiva e alla tecnologia Flash, abbiamo cercato di renderlo un'esperienza in grado d'immergere l'utente nella fotografia. //// Através de uma navegação intuitiva e recorrendo à tecnologia Flash, tentámos criar uma experiência memorável, fazendo com que o visitante se concentre na fotografia.

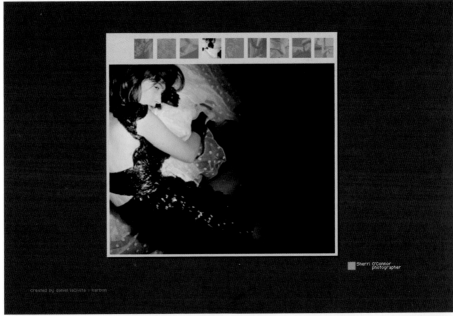

Infos

DESIGN AND PROGRAMMING: Daniel LaCivita (Karbon Studios) <www.karbonstudios.com>. /// AWARDS: FWA. /// TOOLS: Macromedia Flash. ///
COST: 1 week. /// MAINTENANCE: 2 hours per month.

SHOONYA DESIGN

www.shoonyadesign.net

La web Shoonya Design es un porfolio de diseño. Su objetivo primordial es mostrar mi potencial como profesional creativo del ámbito del diseño **gráfico e interactivo.** //// Il sito di Shoonya design è un sito portfolio di design. L'obiettivo principale è dimostrare la mia forza di professionista creativo nel settore dell'interazione e del graphic design. //// **Neste site, a Shoonya design expõe o seu portfólio. O principal objectivo consiste em apresentar a minha capacidade profissional criativa no domínio da interacção/design gráfico.**

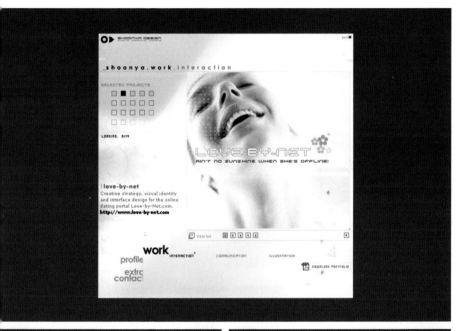

DESIGN AND PROGRAMMING: Shoonya Design. /// **AWARDS:** TAXI (Site of the Week), Americal Design Award, Plasticpilots, DOPE, Golden Web (Site of the Month), Style Boost, NewWebPick (Superpick of the World), Flash Vista, Spoono, etc. /// **TOOLS:** Adobe Photoshop, Macromedia Flash, Macromedia Dreamweaver. /// **COST:** 400 hours.

Concept

Nuestra web sirve a nuestros clientes actuales y potenciales de medio interactivo para producir y entregar porfolios dispuestos en filas y columnas. //// Il nostro sito funziona da mezzo di comunicazione interattivo per i clienti effettivi e potenziali, per produrre e consegnare portfolio a strisce, simili ad una stampa a contatto. //// O nosso site funciona como um meio interactivo para os nossos clientes actuais e futuros, em que são produzidos partes de portfólios semelhantes a um cartão de visita.

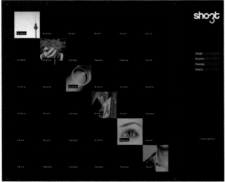

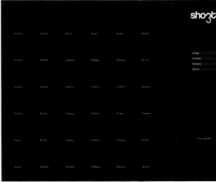

Infos

DESIGN: JF Mayrand and JC Yacono (Epoxy) <www.epoxy.ca>. /// **PROGRAMMING:** François Arbour, Serge Grenier and Julien Fondère. /// **TOOLS:** html, Macromedia Flash, php. /// **COST:** 80 hours.

Concept

El juego constante de luces y sombras determinó la elección del fondo negro y de una estructura gráfica minimalista para que el ojo no se fije en nada más allá de la poesía de las fotografías. //// Il gioco costante delle ombre e delle luci determina la scelta di un fondo nero e di una struttura grafica minimalista in modo che l'occhio possa essere catturato solo dalla poesia delle fotografie. //// O jogo constante entre as sombras e as luzes justifica a escolha de um fundo negro, bem como de uma estrutura gráfica minimalista, para que o olho apenas se concentre na poesia das fotografias.

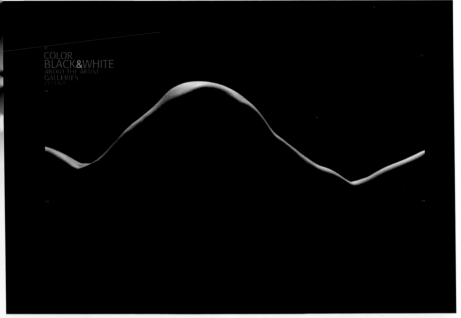

Infos

DESIGN AND PROGRAMMING: UZIK <www.uzik.com>. /// TOOLS: Macromedia Flash, html, php. /// COST: 1 month.

Concept

Alegre, trabajadísima y densa. La web cambia al azar en cada nueva visita. //// Vivace, dedicato e ben strutturato. Il sito cambia in modo casuale a ogni nuova visita. //// Divertida, dedicada e sólida. Em cada visita, o site altera-se aleatoriamente.

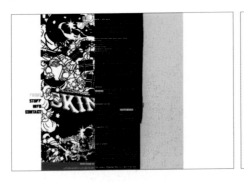 

Infos

DESIGN AND PROGRAMMING: SKIN. /// TOOLS: html. /// COST: 15 hours. /// MAINTENANCE: 3 hours per month.

SKWAKCOLORS

www.skwak.com

FRANCE
2003

Concept

Tan sólo un caos feliz y bastante alocado. //// Nient'altro che un caos allegro e un po' pazzo. //// Simplesmente uma alegre confusão, deveras alucinante.

Infos

DESIGN AND PROGRAMMING: SKWAKCOLORS. /// TOOLS: html, Macromedia Flash. /// COST: 40 hours. /// MAINTENANCE: 10-20 hours per month.

SEAN KENNEDY SANTOS PHOTO

www.sksantos.com

Concept

Contenido basado en las imágenes y acentuado por un enfoque minimalista del diseño (todos los elementos del menú tenían que caber en una página). Tiempo de carga adecuado para dos plataformas. //// Il sito è caratterizzato da un contenuto basato sull'immagine e accentuato da un approccio al design minimalista (tutti gli elementi del menù devono essere su una sola pagina), con un tempo di caricamento opportuno per due piattaforme. //// Conteúdo baseado em imagens e acentuado por uma abordagem minimalista ao design (todos os elementos do menu estão numa página apenas); carregamento apropriado para duas plataformas.

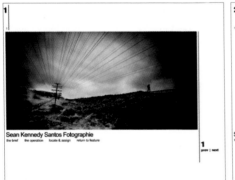

Infos

DESIGN: Eight x Ten. /// PROGRAMMING: Code & Theory <www.codeandtheory.com>. /// AWARDS: One Show, PDN Annual Best Site. /// TOOLS: Macromedia Flash. /// COST: 2 weeks.

SOPPCOLLECTIVE

AUSTRALIA
2002

El bosque de setas y las criaturillas [el equipo] que lo habitan nos vinculan con nuestra identidad, funcionan como elemento lúdico y reflejan el espíritu libre de nuestro colectivo. //// La foresta di funghi e le creature [il team] che la popolano dovrebbero riflettere le nostre identità, funzionare da elemento di svago ed evidenziare la natura libera del nostro gruppo. //// A floresta dos cogumelos e os pequenos seres [a equipa] que nela vivem representam o elo de ligação com a nossa identidade e o trabalho como elemento de diversão; pretendem ainda reflectir a natureza descontraída do nosso colectivo.

DESIGN AND PROGRAMMING: Soppcollective. /// AWARDS: Guinness Young Contemporary Art, Output [Silver]. /// TOOLS: html, Macromedia Flash. /// COST: we wish we'd remember. /// MAINTENANCE: 2 hours per month.

STEPHEN BLISS

www.stephenbliss.com

Concept

Para entretener e informar. //// Intrattenere e informare. //// Para entreter e informar.

Infos

DESIGN AND PROGRAMMING: Futaba Hayashi <www.futabita.com>. /// **AWARDS:** NewWebPick (Site of the Day), FWA (Site of the Day), e-Creative (Site of the Day). /// **TOOLS:** html, Macromedia Flash. /// **COST:** 9 months. /// **MAINTENANCE:** 5 hours per month.

Concept

El visitante no tiene más que sentarse cómodamente, relajarse y... empezar a soñar. //// Il visitatore deve solo sedersi, rilassarsi e... cominciare a sognare. //// O visitante apenas tem que se recostar na cadeira, descontrair e... começar a sonhar.

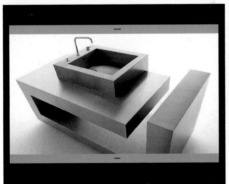

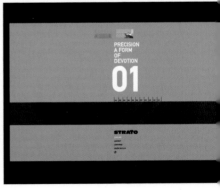

Infos

DESIGN AND PROGRAMMING: group94 <www.group94.com>. /// AWARDS: Bombshock, BestFlashAnimationSite.com (Site of the Week), FWA (Site of the Day) /// TOOLS: Macromedia Flash, php. /// COST: 6 weeks. /// MAINTENANCE: 2 days every year.

Sensualidad y función. //// Glamour e funzionalità. //// Glamour e Função.

DESIGN: Underwaterpistol <www.underwaterpistol.com>. /// PROGRAMMING: Gary Carruthers and Gary Belton. /// TOOLS: html, Macromedia Flash, php, MySQL. /// COST: 270 hours. /// MAINTENANCE: 4 hours per month.

BREAKFAST DESIGN STUD

www.studiobreakfast.com

Concept

La idea consistía en crear una web sencilla para mejorar la visibilidad de nuestros trabajos, con un siste
que es lo más importante del porfolio. //// Il concetto base era realizzare un sito semplice per migliorare la
gradevole e fluida che costituisce il punto di forza del portfolio. //// Pretendemos construir um site simples
trabalhos, com uma navegação boa e fluida, que constitui o aspecto principal deste portfólio.

Infos

DESIGN AND PROGRAMMING: Martin Dellicour [Breakfast]. /// **AWARDS:** Styleboost, Linkdup, Newstoday, etc. /// T
script. /// **COST:** 40 hours to create the actual site. /// **MAINTENANCE:** 2-3 hours per month.

Un estudio de animación cordial. //// Il tuo studio d'animazione amico. //// O seu estúdio de animação amigável.

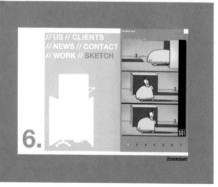

DESIGN: Jakob Schuh and Saschka Unseld (Studio Soi). /// **PROGRAMMING:** Saschka Unseld, Anna Kubik and Sandra Jakisch. /// **TOOLS:** html, Macromedia Flash, film. /// **COST:** 2 weeks. /// **MAINTENANCE:** 15 minutes per month.

Concept

Para crear lo contrario de lo obvio con teorías procedentes de la filosofía del azar y del absurdo. //// Creare l'opposto della banalità coinvolgendo teorie dalla filosofia della casualità e dell'assurdo. //// Para criar o contrário do óbvio, envolvendo teorias baseadas na filosofia do acaso e do nonsense.

Infos

DESIGN AND PROGRAMMING: Andrew Cross (Super 8). /// TOOLS: Macromedia Flash, html, GIFs, MP3. /// MAINTENANCE: 48 hours a month.

Concept

El reto: presentar el porfolio de producción de audio de Tesis con eficacia, crear un sitio que reflejara algo de la personalidad de la empresa y convertirlo en una grata experiencia. //// Le nostre sfide: presentare in modo efficace l'eccezionale portfolio della produzione audio di Tesis, creare un sito caratteristico capace di rivelare una parte della personalità dell'azienda e rendere il tutto un'esperienza divertente. //// Os nossos desafios: apresentar de forma efectiva o incrível portfólio no domínio da produção áudio, criar um site distintivo que revela algo da personalidade da empresa e transformá-lo numa experiência agradável.

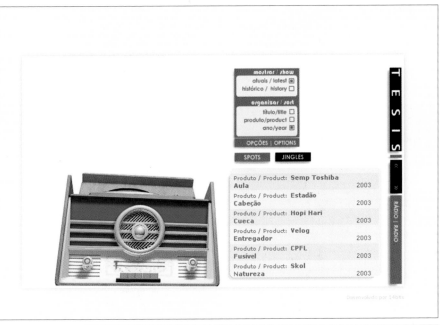

DESIGN AND PROGRAMMING: 14bits Produções <www.14bits.com.br >. /// TOOLS: Macromedia Flash, 3D, php, pencil, video, film, music. /// COST: 500 hours from briefing to publishing. /// MAINTENANCE: there is no maintenance costs because Tesis updates the entire site via a content management system.

TETSOO PRODUCTION

www.tetsoo.com

Concept

Quería una interfaz muy austera y práctica, mejorada con animaciones 3D integradas en la navegación general. //// Ho scelto un'interfaccia molto chiara e pratica migliorata con animazioni 3D integrate nella navigazione generale. //// Quis conceber um interface muito claro e prático, completado com animações em 3D integradas na navegação geral.

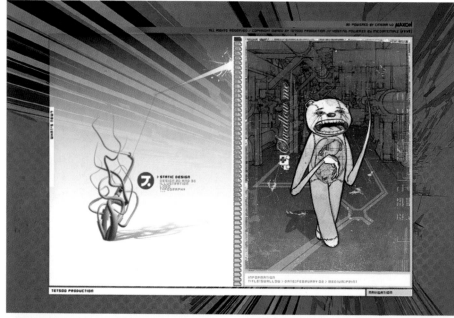

Infos

DESIGN AND PROGRAMMING: Grégoire Poget (Tetsoo). /// **AWARDS:** Bombshock, FWA, e-Creative. /// **TOOLS:** Macromedia Flash, Adobe Photoshop, Adobe Illustrator, Cinema 4D, Adobe AfterEffects, Reason. /// **COST:** 2-3 weeks. /// **MAINTENANCE:** almost zero.

Concept

Simplicidad en estado puro. //// Semplicità pura. //// **Simplicidade pura.**

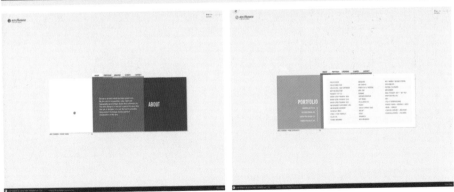

Infos

DESIGN AND PROGRAMMING: Bartłomiej Rozbicki. //// **AWARDS:** fcukstar.com, Netdiver, FWA, BombShok, NewWebPick, TAXI, 4EFX, TINY, Flash Kit, Plasticpilots, American Design Award, etc. /// **TOOLS:** Macromedia Flash, xml, html, music /// **COST:** it's hard to say.

THE LINEAR

www.thelinear.com

Concept

Una web creada para reflejar que The Linear es la mayor urbanización de Singapur. El sistema de navegación permite «fluir» de sección en sección y transmite calma y tranquilidad. //// Un sito che s'ispira nel Linear, il palazzo più lungo di Singapore. La navigazione si caratterizza come un'esperienza continua: ogni sezione "scorre" nella successiva. //// Um site que se centra no Linear, o condomínio mais comprido de Singapura. A navegação apresenta uma experiência contínua em que cada secção "flutua" a caminho da seguinte.

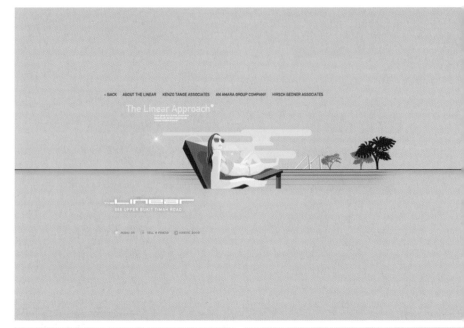

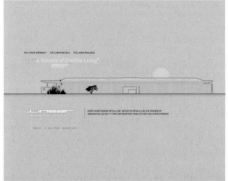
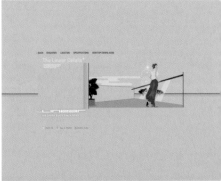

Infos

DESIGN: Kinetic Interactive <www.kinetic.com.sg>. /// **PROGRAMMING:** Benjy Choo. /// **AWARDS:** Young Guns, Singapore Creative Circle. /// **TOOLS:** html, Macromedia Flash, php. /// **COST:** 120 hours. /// **MAINTENANCE:** none.

Concept El objetivo era obtener una página amena y sencilla a la vez, por la que se pudiera navegar rápido y sin complicaciones. //// Lo scopo era realizzare una pagina web divertente e chiara per navigare velocemente e senza ostacoli. Il sito contiene animazioni flash non invasive che rimangono sullo sfondo e non competono a livello delle illustrazioni ma che, tuttavia, conferiscono al tutto un piacere estetico. //// O objectivo consistiu em criar um página divertida e arrumada, para que se pudesse navegar rapidamente e de uma forma pouco complicada.

DESIGN: Uli Oesterle. /// **PROGRAMMING:** Matthis Herrmann. /// **AWARDS:** FWA, Turkey Awards. /// **TOOLS:** Adobe Photoshop, Adobe Illustrator, Macromedia Flash. /// **COST:** 110 hours. /// **MAINTENANCE:** 4-20 hours per month.

Concept

Investigue, mezcle y observe. Experimentará thepharmacy. //// Esplorate, mescolate e osservate gli esperimenti di thepharmacy. ////
Explore, misture e observe, de forma a passar pela experiência da thepharmacy.

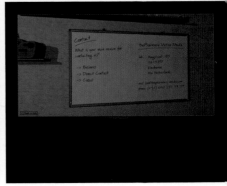

Infos

DESIGN: thePharmacy. /// **PROGRAMMING:** F. Litjens and J. Kessels. /// **AWARDS:** FWA. /// **TOOLS:** Macromedia Flash, Discreet 3D Studio Max, Adobe Photoshop.
/// **COST:** 100 hours divided over 2 months. /// **MAINTENANCE:** if ever, 2 hours per month.

Concept

Maravillosos gráficos con sutiles animaciones. El visitante es quien pone en marcha el vídeo nada más entrar en la web. Sin reproductores externos. Formatos flexibles (aleatorios) 4:3 y 16:9. Fácil de actualizar. //// Grafica favolosa e abile animazione. Si dà subito il via allo showreel fin dall'entrata nel sito. Nessun video player esterno. Formati flessibili (random) a 4:3 e 16:9. Facile da aggiornare. //// Gráficos esplêndidos com animações subtis. Accionar a bobina do show. Começar a acção logo que se entra no site. Sem vídeos externos. Formatos 4:3 e 16:9 flexíveis (aleatório). Actualização simples.

DESIGN: Twisted Interactive <www.twisted.nl>. /// PROGRAMMING: Dennis Danen. /// AWARDS: Linkdup, Styleboost, Uailab (Site of the Month), and various other notifications. /// TOOLS: Macromedia Flash, xml, php, video. /// COST: 3 weeks. /// MAINTENANCE: Depending on the amount of video- or animationprojects developed by The Village. Clips are uploaded via CMS.

Concept

Una alegre fuente de inspiración para la moda. //// Una vivace fonte d'ispirazione di fashion. //// **Divertida fonte de inspiração para moda.**

Infos

DESIGN AND PROGRAMMING: Are Bu Vindenes <www.arervindenes.com>. /// **TOOLS:** Macromedia Flash, html. /// **COST:** 100 hours.

TIM MITCHELL
www.t-mitchell.com

USA
2004

Concept

Una web para presentar a los fotógrafos de este agente de forma clásica y clara, con un diseño distintivo que hace que destaque entre sitios similares. //// Il sito presenta i fotografi in modo chiaro e classico con un design distintivo per separare ciascuno di loro dagli altri. //// Apresenta os fotógrafos da agência de uma forma clássica e clara, com um design distintivo que sobressai em relação aos restantes sites.

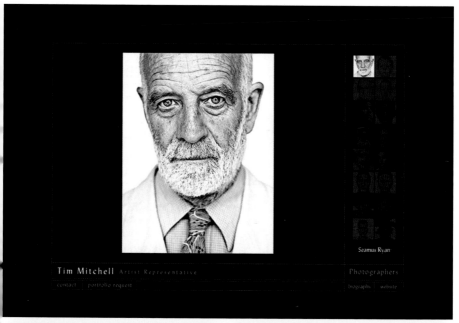

DESIGN: Chris Christodoulou (Saddington & Baynes) <www.sb-showcase.com>. /// PROGRAMMING: Duncan Hart. /// TOOLS: html, Macromedia Flash.

TOKIDOKI

www.tokidoki.it

Concept

Tokidoki empezó siendo mi diario artístico personal, un lugar donde mostrar mi arte y mi alma, una casa para que la habitaran mis personajes. Ahora es una marca. //// Tokidoki è cominciato come il mio diario artistico personale, dove mostrare la mia arte e la mia anima, un luogo con caratteri vivi. Ora è una marca. //// O Tokidoki começou por ser o meu diário artístico pessoal, um meio para expor a minha arte e a minha alma, uma casa em que os seus habitantes têm vida. Actualmente, é uma marca.

Infos

DESIGN: Simone Legno (TOKIDOKI). /// **PROGRAMMING:** Emanuele Petrungaro and Simone Legno. /// **AWARDS:** Flash Film Festival New York, Flash Film Festival San Francisco, SXSW Interactive in Austin, FWA. /// **TOOLS:** Adobe Illustrator, Macromedia Flash, xml, php, html, music. /// **COST:** continuous update. /// **MAINTENANCE:** doesn't need maintenance, exept adding news or eventual little updates.

Concept

Sin tiempos de carga demasiado largos, sin una navegación demasiado complicada: una web divertida y con buenos contenidos. //// Gli evito delle attese troppo lunghe per caricare la pagina, nonché una navigazione troppo complicata, ma può surfare in maniera divertente e trovare buoni contenuti. //// Sem períodos de carregamento longos e não tendo uma navegação muito complicada, este site dá-lhe a garantia de que aqui irá divertir-se a surfar e descobrir um conteúdo de grande qualidade.

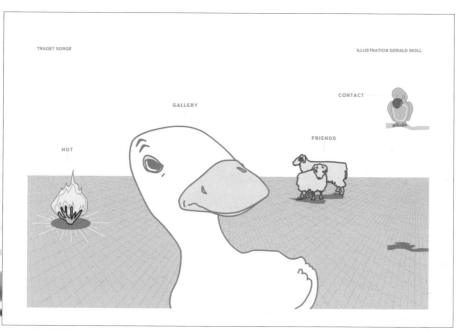

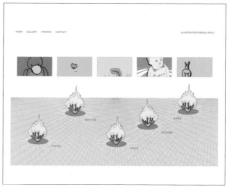

Intos

DESIGN: Gerald Moll (Traget Sorge). /// **PROGRAMMING:** Ralf Boller <ww.platzhalter.com >. /// **TOOLS:** Macromedia Flash, music, Adobe Image Ready, movies. /// **COST:** 111 hours, and a bar of cigarettes. /// **MAINTENANCE:** never counted them.

Concept

Crear un sitio web rápido para 15 fotógrafos. //// Un sito di veloce consultazione per 15 fotografi. //// Criar um site rápido para 15 fotógrafos.

Infos

DESIGN: Struktour <www.struktour.de>. /// PROGRAMMING: Katharina Moelle. /// TOOLS: Macromedia Flash. /// COST: 65 hours ///
MAINTENANCE: 2 hours per month.

UNREAL

www.unreal-uk.com

Concept

La idea básica consistía en centrarnos en la razón por la que nos visitan: averiguar qué es lo que hacemos o decimos y cómo ponerse en contacto con nosotros. A partir de ahí, nuestra web se convierte en una plataforma sencilla y accesible. //// L'idea da sviluppare era di focalizzarsi sul motivo per cui il visitatore entra nel sito: per vedere ciò che facciamo e diciamo e come tenerci stretti. Ecco quindi una piattaforma semplice e accessibile per raggiungere lo scopo. //// Centrámo-nos na motivação do visitante para aceder a este site: para ver o que fazemos/dizemos e para nos contactar. Desta forma, torna-se uma plataforma simples e acessível.

Infos

DESIGN: Brian Eagle and Matt Barnes (Unreal). /// PROGRAMMING: Matt Barnes. /// TOOLS: Macromedia Flash, dhtml. /// COST: 20 hours. /// MAINTENANCE: 2 hours.

VIAGRAFIK

www.viagrafik.com

Concept

Variedad. //// Varietà. //// Variedade.

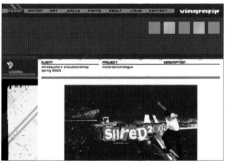 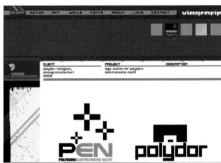

Infos

DESIGN AND PROGRAMMING: Viagrafik. /// TOOLS: Macromedia Flash, html, php, JavaScript, music, film. /// COST: 120 hours. /// MAINTENANCE: 5 hours per month.

URBANSOLDIERZ

www.urbansoldierz.com

Concept

La web está inspirada en diseños urbanos. //// Il sito è ispirato ai disegni urbani. //// O site inspira-se no design urbano.

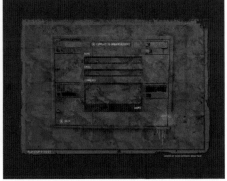

Infos

DESIGN AND PROGRAMMING: Jordi Oró Solé (Medusateam) <www.medusateam.com>. /// **AWARDS:** Plasticpilots. /// **TOOLS:** html, Macromedia Flash, Adobe Photoshop. /// **COST:** 3 months. /// **MAINTENANCE:** 3-5 days per month.

VERNE PHOTOGRAPHY

www.verne.be

Concept

El sistema de navegación nos recuerda con inteligencia que estamos en Internet al tiempo que nos envuelve en una relajante mezcla de música de
cítara y de yoga. //// Il sistema di navigazione suscita in modo intelligente un gusto on-line mentre si è circondati da una rilassante miscela di musica
yoga. //// Envolvido por uma compilação tranquilizante de música de cítara e ioga, o sistema de navegação conduz-nos através do site de uma
forma inteligente.

Infos

DESIGN AND PROGRAMMING: group94 <www.group94.com>. /// TOOLS: Macromedia Flash, php. /// COST: 3 weeks. /// MAINTENANCE: 1-2 days every year.

VIADUCT

www.viaduct.co.uk

Concept

El usuario puede filtrar la búsqueda por diseñador, material, tipo de mueble y fabricante. Para desplazarse por la lista de resultados, es suficiente con arrastrar el ratón por la pantalla. //// Grazie al filtraggio delle richieste degli utenti in base a designer, materiali, tipi di contenuti e fabbricanti, ogni ricerca è in grado di creare un'ampia gamma di prodotti che è possibile sfogliare muovendo il canvas sullo schermo. //// As diferentes secções, organizadas por designers, materiais, tipos de mobília e produtores, filtram a procura, dando acesso a uma selecção de produtos, como se se estivesse a mover a tela dentro do ecrã.

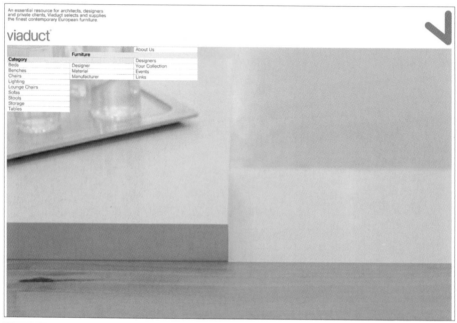

Infos

DESIGN AND PROGRAMMING: de-construct <www.de-construct.com>. /// TOOLS: Macromedia Flash, xml, music. /// COST: 7 weeks.

VIK MUNIZ
www.vikmuniz.net

Concept

La idea era crear un flujo de datos que ordenara cronológicamente textos e imágenes. Se buscaba que la información resultara accesible y directa.
//// L'idea era creare un flusso d'informazioni che includesse testi e immagini disposti in ordine cronologico e che fosse diretto e facilmente accessibile.
//// A ideia consistiu na criação de um fluxo de informação, incluindo textos e imagens organizados cronologicamente. Pretendeu-se tornar esta informação acessível e directa.

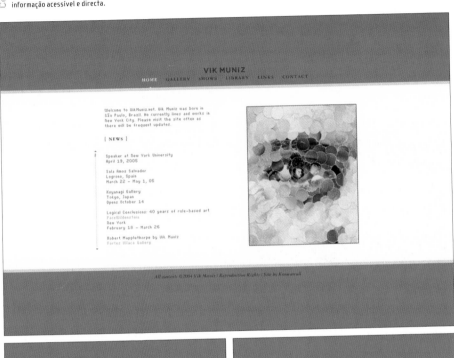

Infos

DESIGN AND PROGRAMMING: Knowawall Design <www.knowawall.com>. /// TOOLS: Macromedia Flash, html. /// COST: 90 hours. ///
MAINTENANCE: 5 hours per month.

VILLA EUGÉNIE

www.villaeugenie.com

Concept

Dinámicos pases de diapositivas y espectáculos multimedia personalizados constituyen el núcleo de esta innovadora web. //// Slide show dinamiche e presentazioni multimediali personalizzate rappresentano l'anima di questo sito web innovativo. //// Shows de slides dinâmicos e shows de multimédia adaptados a cada cliente constituem o núcleo deste site inovador.

villa eugénie

villa eugénie
t +32 (0)2 5430060
f +32 (0)2 5387225
info@villaeugenie.com

Enter

villa eugénie

WHO WE ARE

Our favourites

Activities
Clients

Recent work   Contact

RENTALS
プレスリリース

Infos

DESIGN: Basedesign <www.basedesign.com>, Tentwelve <www.tentwelve.com> and Villa Eugénie. /// **PROGRAMMING:** Tentwelve. ///
TOOLS: Macromedia Flash, php, html, MySQL. /// **COST:** sorry, no idea. /// **MAINTENANCE:** programmer side: 1 hour per month; client: 50 hours.

Concept

Sé moderno, sé divertido, sé adaptable. //// Forte, divertente, agevole. //// Sê cool, sê engraçado, sê sofisticado.

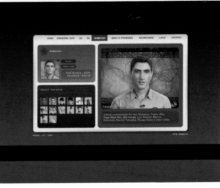

Infos

DESIGN: Vitor Vilela and Marcus Silva (GiantHouse Broadband Team). /// **PROGRAMMING:** Marcus Silva. /// **AWARDS:** FWA (Site of the Day), 4EFX (Site of the Month), Bombshock, Gold Site (Best Animation Flash), Netdiver, TAXI, XsiBase, TINY, and many others. /// **TOOLS:** html, Macromedia Flash, Quicktime, JavaScript. /// **COST:** 4 weeks.

BEN VULKERS PHOTO

THE NETHERLANDS

www.vulkersfotografie.nl

2002

Concept

Una navegación directa y un aspecto gráfico (mínimo) que dirijan toda la atención hacia las fotografías. Que el fotógrafo pueda gestionar los contenidos en su totalidad. //// La navigazione lineare e la veste grafica (essenziale) intendono accompagnare lo sguardo a focalizzarsi sulle immagini. I contenuti devono poter essere maneggiati completamente dallo stesso fotografo. //// Uma navegação fácil de compreender e elementos gráficos (minimalistas) que dirigem para o centro fulcral: as fotografias. Os conteúdos podem ser completamente geridos pelo próprio fotógrafo.

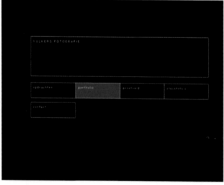

Infos

DESIGN AND PROGRAMMING: Henk Gruppen (Gruppen Grafische Vormgeving). /// TOOLS: Macromedia Flash, plain FTP-based CMS. /// COST: 20-30 hours. /// MAINTENANCE: 2 hours per month.

WARREN HEISE ILLUSTRATION CANADA

www.warrenheise.com
2003

Concept

El diseño es como un collage a base de papeles, adhesivos y textos escritos a máquina. Está hecho con colores neutros y con una animación sutil que subrayan las obras. //// Il design è come un collage, con pezzetti di carta, colle e testi scritti a macchina. Per dare una maggiore enfasi al lavoro uso dei colori neutri e una leggera animazione. //// O design foi concebido como uma colagem, com pedaços de papel, autocolantes e texto escrito à máquina. As cores neutrais e a animação subtil visam realçar o trabalho apresentado.

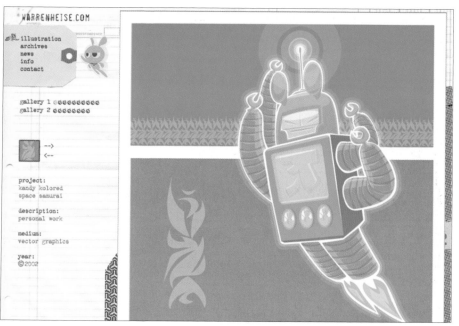

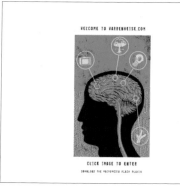

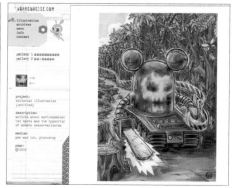

Infos

DESIGN AND PROGRAMMING: Warren Heise. /// AWARDS: Netdiver Design Forte, VisualOrgasmus (Artist of the Month). /// TOOLS: html, Macromedia Flash. /// COST: 150 hours. /// MAINTENANCE: 4 hours per month.

WINTHERS WONDER WORLD

www.wintherswonderworld.com

Concept

Una web interactiva que invita al visitante a explorar el maravilloso mundo de Winther. //// Un sito interattivo che invita lo spettatore ad esplorare il Paese delle Meraviglie di Winther. //// Um site interactivo que convida os visitantes a explorar o Winderworld de Winther.

Infos

DESIGN: Pierre Winther. /// PROGRAMMING: Malthe Sigurdsson. /// TOOLS: Macromedia Flash. /// COST: 180-200 hours. /// MAINTENANCE: 10 hours per month.

WISHART DESIGN

Concept

Sencilla, funcional y fácil de navegar. //// *Semplice, funzionale e di facile navigazione.* //// **Simples, funcional e de fácil navegação.**

www.wishartdesign.com

DESIGN: Zoe Wishart and Dan Ellis (Wishart Design). /// **PROGRAMMING:** Jason Stevenson. /// **TOOLS:** Macromedia Flash. /// **COST:** 3 weeks. /// **MAINTENANCE:** 4 hours per month.

YRMIS

www.yrmis.com

Concept

Las prendas son la interfaz; la interfaz son las prendas. //// *I vestiti sono l'interfaccia e l'interfaccia sono i vestiti.* //// **As roupas são o intermediário, o intermediário é as roupas.**

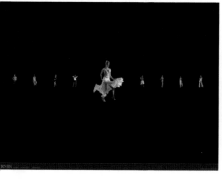 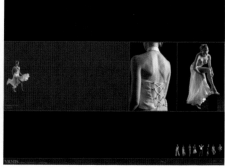

DESIGN AND PROGRAMMING: Knowawall Design <www.knowawall.com>. /// **AWARDS:** TINY. /// **TOOLS:** Macromedia Flash, html. /// **COST:** 90 hours. /// **MAINTENANCE:** 2 hours per month.

DEAN ZILLWOOD PHOTO   NEW ZEALAND

www.zillwood.co.nz   2003

Concept

Para evitar el vacío de algunos sitios web minimalistas, le pusimos una música neozelandesa que aporta sabor y personalidad. //// Per evitare la sterilità di alcuni siti troppo essenziali, abbiamo inserito musica neozelandese, aggiungendo così un tocco di gusto e di personalità. //// Para evitar a esterilidade que caracteriza alguns sites minimalistas e lhe conferir mais tempero e personalidade, adicionámos música neozelandesa.

Infos

DESIGN: Native <www.nativehome.com>. /// PROGRAMMING: Spencer Levine and Toshi Endo. /// TOOLS: Macromedia Flash, html. /// COST: 20 hours. /// MAINTENANCE: 1 hour per month.

ZTAMPZ

www.ztampz.com

Concept

«Zelloz». //// "ztamptare". //// "ztamping".

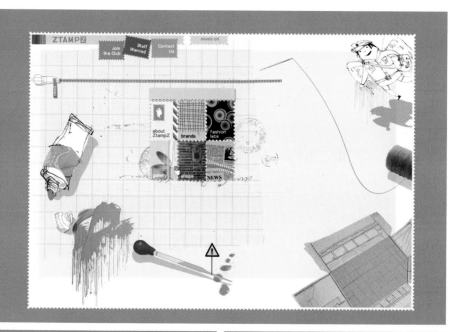

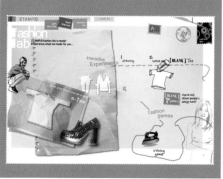

DESIGN AND PROGRAMMING: rice 5 <www.rice5.com>. /// **TOOLS:** html, Macromedia Flash, xml. /// **COST:** 1 month.

TASCHEN is not responsible when web addresses cannot be reached if they are offline or can be viewed just with plug-ins.

I would like to thank all studios and professionals participating in the book, as well all people involved, for their contribution and effort to provide the materials and information that enriched this publication. Also Daniel Siciliano Bretas for his tireless work contacting all the offices we wanted to include in this book and for his work designing and layouting the book. His work has been fundamental to make this a great inspirational series. Moreover, Stefan Klatte for guiding us always in the technical details and helping us making a better job every day.

Web Design: Portfolios

To stay informed about upcoming TASCHEN titles,
please request our magazine at www.taschen.com
or write to TASCHEN, Hohenzollernring 53,
D–50672 Cologne, Germany, Fax: +49-221-254919.
We will be happy to send you a free copy of our magazine
which is filled with information about all of our books.

Design: Daniel Siciliano Brêtas
Layout: Daniel Siciliano Brêtas & Julius Wiedemann
Production: Stefan Klatte

Editor: Julius Wiedemann
Assitant-editor: Daniel Siciliano Brêtas
French Translation: Anna Guillerm
German Translation: Heike Lohneis
Spanish Translation: Raquel Valle
Italian Translation: Olivia Papili
Portuguese Translation: Ricardo Esteves Correia

Printed in Italy
ISBN-13: 978-3-8228-4044-3
ISBN-10: 3-8228-4044-0

Web Design: E-Commerce
Ed. Julius Wiedemann /
Flexi-cover, 192 pp. / € 6.99 /
$ 9.99 / £ 4.99 / ¥ 1.500

Web Design: Flash Sites
Ed. Julius Wiedemann /
Flexi-cover, 192 pp. / € 6.99 /
$ 9.99 / £ 4.99 / ¥ 1.500

Web Design: Music Sites
Ed. Julius Wiedemann /
Flexi-cover, 192 pp. / € 6.99 /
$ 9.99 / £ 4.99 / ¥ 1.500

"These books are beautiful objects, well-designed and lucid." —*Le Monde*, Paris, on the ICONS series

"Buy them all and add some pleasure to your life."

African Style
Ed. Angelika Taschen

Alchemy & Mysticism
Alexander Roob

American Indian
Dr. Sonja Schierle

Angels
Gilles Néret

Architecture Now!
Ed. Philip Jodidio

Art Now
Eds. Burkhard Riemschneider,
Uta Grosenick

Atget's Paris
Ed. Hans Christian Adam

Audrey Hepburn
Ed. Paul Duncan

Bamboo Style
Ed. Angelika Taschen

Berlin Style
Ed. Angelika Taschen

Brussels Style
Ed. Angelika Taschen

Cars of the 50s
Ed. Jim Heimann, Tony Thacker

Cars of the 60s
Ed. Jim Heimann, Tony Thacker

Cars of the 70s
Ed. Jim Heimann, Tony Thacker

Chairs
Charlotte & Peter Fiell

Charlie Chaplin
Ed. Paul Duncan

China Style
Ed. Angelika Taschen

Christmas
Ed. Jim Heimann, Steven Heller

Classic Rock Covers
Ed. Michael Ochs

Clint Eastwood
Ed. Paul Duncan

Design Handbook
Charlotte & Peter Fiell

Design of the 20th Century
Charlotte & Peter Fiell

Design for the 21st Century
Charlotte & Peter Fiell

Devils
Gilles Néret

Digital Beauties
Ed. Julius Wiedemann

Robert Doisneau
Ed. Jean-Claude Gautrand

East German Design
Ralf Ulrich / Photos: Ernst Hedler

Egypt Style
Ed. Angelika Taschen

Encyclopaedia Anatomica
Ed. Museo La Specola Florence

M.C. Escher

Fashion
Ed. The Kyoto Costume Institute

Fashion Now!
Ed. Terry Jones, Susie Rushton

Fruit
Ed. George Brookshaw,
Uta Pellgrü-Gagel

HR Giger
HR Giger

Grand Tour
Harry Seidler

Graphic Design
Eds. Charlotte & Peter Fiell

Greece Style
Ed. Angelika Taschen

Halloween
Ed. Jim Heimann, Steven Heller

Havana Style
Ed. Angelika Taschen

Homo Art
Gilles Néret

Hot Rods
Ed. Coco Shinomiya, Tony
Thacker

Hula
Ed. Jim Heimann

Indian Style
Ed. Angelika Taschen

India Bazaar
Samantha Harrison, Bari Kumar

Industrial Design
Charlotte & Peter Fiell

Japanese Beauties
Ed. Alex Gross

Las Vegas
Ed. Jim Heimann,
W. R. Wilkerson III

London Style
Ed. Angelika Taschen

Marilyn Monroe
Ed. Paul Duncan

Marlon Brando
Ed. Paul Duncan

Mexico Style
Ed. Angelika Taschen

Miami Style
Ed. Angelika Taschen

Minimal Style
Ed. Angelika Taschen

Morocco Style
Ed. Angelika Taschen

New York Style
Ed. Angelika Taschen

Orson Welles
Ed. Paul Duncan

Paris Style
Ed. Angelika Taschen

Penguin
Frans Lanting

20th Century Photography
Museum Ludwig Cologne

Photo Icons I
Hans-Michael Koetzle

Photo Icons II
Hans-Michael Koetzle

Pierre et Gilles
Eric Troncy

Provence Style
Ed. Angelika Taschen

Robots & Spaceships
Ed. Teruhisa Kitahara

Safari Style
Ed. Angelika Taschen

Seaside Style
Ed. Angelika Taschen

Signs
Ed. Julius Wiedeman

South African Style
Ed. Angelika Taschen

Starck
Philippe Starck

Surfing
Ed. Jim Heimann

Sweden Style
Ed. Angelika Taschen

Sydney Style
Ed. Angelika Taschen

Tattoos
Ed. Henk Schiffmacher

Tiffany
Jacob Baal-Teshuva

Tiki Style
Sven Kirsten

Tokyo Style
Ed. Angelika Taschen

Tuscany Style
Ed. Angelika Taschen

Valentines
Ed. Jim Heimann,
Steven Heller

Web Design: Best Studios
Ed. Julius Wiedemann

Web Design: E-Commerce
Ed. Julius Wiedemann

Web Design: Flash Sites
Ed. Julius Wiedemann

Web Design: Music Sites
Ed. Julius Wiedemann

Web Design: Portfolios
Ed. Julius Wiedemann

**Women Artists
in the 20th and 21st Century**
Ed. Uta Grosenick

70s Style
Ed. Jim Heimann

ICONS